From Farms to Foreign Markets

NIPA® GENX ELECTRONIC RESOURCES & SOLUTIONS P. LTD.
New Delhi-110 034

About the Editors

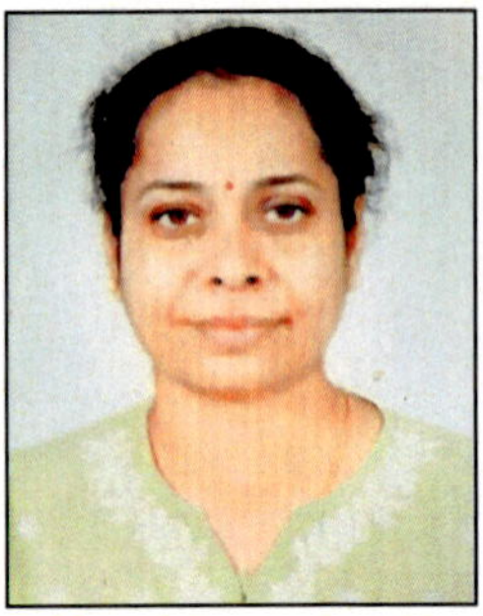

Dr. Ritambhara Singh is currently serving as Associate Professor (Agribusiness Management), at the School of Agribusiness and Rural Management in Dr Rajendra Prasad Central Agricultural University, India. A highly accomplished academic, she holds a Master's and a Doctorate in Agricultural Economics from Govind Ballabh Pant University of Agriculture and Technology, India and various Certificates from the Universities of Michigan, and Illinois, USA, as also from the University of Adelaide, Australia. She was one of the participants in Sathguru Cornell's Food and Agribusiness Executive Management Program, 2022 as offered by Cornell University, USA. Her professional experience of around 20 years spans across reputed organizations - ICAR-Indian Agricultural Research Institute, New Delhi, MCX India Ltd, Mumbai, Advanced Biofuels USA, Maryland, USA, FAS-USDA, US Embassy, New Delhi, Compound Livestock Feed Manufacturers Association, Mumbai, and Anand Agricultural University, India. She is currently engaged in the teaching of P. G., and Ph.D. courses in the programs of Agribusiness Management, Rural Management, and Agricultural Economics, as well as guiding them in their research work. She has handled various National and International Projects funded by UNCTAD, World Bank- ICAR, the Government of Gujarat, The Securities and Exchange Board of India, ICSSR, and many more. Amidst her repertoire of academic interests across the canvas of Economics and Business Management, International Trade, Producer Collectives, Circular and Bioeconomy and Secondary Agriculture have been her passion. Since 2019, she has engaged with this domain through organisation of workshops, summer camps, project research, guiding of students' research, and publication of various articles and a book. She has won several awards including that of Excellence in reporting by the US Department of Agriculture. She is a member of several professional bodies and is on the editorial board of magazines. She has more than 190 publications to her credit in various forms in reputed journals, magazines, and news dailies. She is currently the Principal Investigator of a University funded project on Business Environment Analysis for Secondary Agriculture in India, a project director in ICSSR funded collaborative project on the concept of nutri gardens, a Government of Bihar funded project on impact assessment of CRA technologies and is CO-PI in All India Coordinated Research Project on small millets and Government of Bihar funded Centre of Excellence in Millets and value chain under fourth Krishi Roadmap of Bihar.

Dr. A.R. Shravanthi is an Assistant Professor at the School of Agribusiness and Rural Management, Dr. Rajendra Prasad Central Agricultural University, Bihar, bringing over six years of teaching and research experience. She educates both postgraduate and undergraduate students in agribusiness, entrepreneurship, and rural management, specializing in areas such as supply chain management, value chains, and production and operations management. Her research interests focus on cold storage warehouse management, small millet value chains, and the promotion of agripreneurship and agricultural startups.

Dr. Shravanthi has made substantial contributions to the field, publishing a variety of scholarly works, including research articles, books, book chapters, manuals, and popular articles in esteemed national and international journals. She has edited influential works such as *Agricultural Sustainability: Strategies for Organic, Climate-Smart, and Resource-Conserving Farming*, which highlights sustainable agriculture, and *Income Augmentation through Small Agribusinesses*, which addresses agripreneurship. Her excellence has been recognized through honors like the Young Scientist Award and the Best Teacher Award.

In addition to her research, Dr. Shravanthi plays a key role in mentoring MBA students, overseeing university-funded projects, and nurturing entrepreneurial skills through her involvement with the Agri-Innovation and Incubation Centre. Her editorial work with e-newsletters and active participation in conferences further demonstrate her dedication to advancing agribusiness and empowering rural communities.

From Farms to Foreign Markets Exploring India's Agricultural Export Transformation

Ritambhara Singh
Associate Professor
(Agribusiness Management)
School of Agribusiness and Rural Management
Dr Rajendra Prasad Central Agricultural University
Smastipur, Pusa, Bihar 848125, India

A.R. Shravanthi
Assistant Professor
School of Agribusiness and Rural Management
Dr. Rajendra Prasad Central Agricultural University
Smastipur, Pusa, Bihar 848125, India

NIPA® GENX ELECTRONIC RESOURCES & SOLUTIONS P. LTD.
New Delhi-110 034

NIPA® GENX ELECTRONIC RESOURCES & SOLUTIONS P. LTD.

101,103, Vikas Surya Plaza, CU Block
L.S.C.Market, Pitam Pura, New Delhi-110 034
Ph : +91 11 4386 0225, 9717133558, 9540816132
E-mail: newindiapublishingagency@gmail.com
Website: www.niparesources.com

Print ISBN: 978-93-58878-46-2

ebook ISBN: 978-93-58879-46-9

Composed and Designed by NIPA®.

Acknowledgement

We are thankful to all the authors for picking up relevant topics for this book. A sincere token of thanks goes to the Vice-Chancellor, Dr. Rajendra Prasad Central Agricultural University, for his persistent encouragement, and focus on Agri-Exports.

We are also thankful to all stakeholders engaged in agricultural supply and value chains. At last, we express gratitude to the publisher, NIPA® Genx Electronic Resources & Solutions P. LTD. at New Delhi for publishing this work

Editors

Preface

Agricultural Export from India is 2.5 percent of the global agricultural trade, while its share in India's merchandise exports is around 10 percent. India's Agriculture Export Policy 2018 aimed at increasing agriculture exports to the tune of 60 billion plus by 2022. i.e. double within a period of five years. In 2022-23, the country exported worth USD 53.1 billion of agricultural goods, with APEDA's share of more than 50 percent. Fresh fruits and processed vegetables were stand out performers registering a growth of 29 percent and 24 percent respectively over the previous year. However, in 2023-24, the exports valued at USD 48.77 billion and in 2024-25, it further fell down to USD 36.95 billion, which could be a concern to many exporters and engaging stakeholders. Does that mean India's agricultural products are losing their competitiveness?

There are several challenges that impede the growth, and competitiveness of agricultural exports from India. There are diseconomies of scale that filter into the cost of production and reduce competitiveness. Post harvest losses are not preventable as the country lacks an efficient cold chain infrastructure and dedicated cold chain transport corridors which further escalates costs, and impacts competitiveness. The lands are fragmented and adoption of technologies is challenging across farms. This leads to variation in quality and quantity of produce from farm to farm. The volume of production is small and for all farms together, thus there are large variations. The International market looks for homogenous volumes and qualities. As a result, exportable homogenous surpluses are not available for several commodities. Disintegrated markets, fragmented supply chains, large number of intermediaries in agricultural markets, and a poor traceability mechanism, non adherence to good agricultural practices are some of the challenges that have impacted the export potential of Indian agriculture. There have been incidences of successive rejection of agricultural products at foreign ports due to breach of Maximum permissible limits of contaminants and residues in different products. Sanitary and Phytosanitary measures have caused s setback to a sustainable export base of agricultural commodities from India. Another key hindrance is in terms low investment in agricultural research and development. While the world is adapting to digital measures and artificial intelligence, India needs to go a long way. Adherence to good agricultural practices is the key. Moreover, land reforms are needed as fragmentation alone has

In the current World of tariff wars, enhancing competitiveness is more important. India must navigate through the agricultural ecosystem in a way that the challenges are addressed at the highest priority level. This book is solely meant for undergraduate and post graduate students to give them a flair of agricultural exports from India via some commodity cases. While there are several research works for one to get a deeper understanding, we do not see many consolidated works, handy enough for young graduates. The book presents a comprehensive and interdisciplinary examination of India's agricultural export landscape, capturing its dynamic evolution, policy support, regional potential and commodity-specific trends woven in ten chapters.

The book begins by laying a global and national context of agri-export performance, followed by a focused analysis of Bihar, one of the lowest farm household income states in the country. The state has substantial agrarian capacity yet it is unutilized along with an under-realized export potential. This regional lens is complemented by commodity-specific studies on fresh and dried grapes and castor, which demonstrates India's comparative advantages, market trajectories, and trade competitiveness in these commodities. However, India also imports grapes. Critical policy initiatives are discussed to understand export landscape, and the challenges posed by non-tariff barriers like SPS and TBT measures, underscoring the need for harmonization, and traceability.

A unique feature of this work is the emphasis on empowering grassroots stakeholders. The chapter on Farmer Producer Organizations (FPOs) highlights the transformative potential of collective action in enhancing international market access for smallholders. Through empirical rigor and policy foresight, the book serves as a valuable resource for undergraduate students and researchers.

Editors

Contents

1

Exploring Agricultural Exports: Current Trends, Status, and Future Prospects

Suresh Chandra Sharma

C.C.S. National Institute of Agricultural Marketing (NIAM)
Bambala, Kota Road, Jaipur-302033, Rajasthan

Abstract

This chapter presents a comprehensive exploration of global agricultural exports, focusing on their pivotal role in economic development, food security, and sustainability. It highlights the growing importance of emerging markets, technological advancements, and evolving consumer preferences such as the rising demand for organic, sustainable and value-added products. An in-depth analysis reveals that agricultural exports contribute significantly to job creation, income generation, and international trade relations, particularly for developing nations. The chapter evaluates India's performance as both an exporter and importer, emphasizing key products like marine goods, rice, spices, and buffalo meat. It further discusses India's engagement with international trade agreements, quality and safety standards, and the challenges and opportunities in maintaining compliance. The future Outlook identifies high-potential sectors including functional, organic, and plant based foods especially in Asia-Pacific, Africa and Latin America. Drawing on data-driven insights, the chapter offers strategic directions for policy makers, agribusiness, and exporters to enhance market access and competitiveness. Overall, it underscores the transformative potential of agricultural trade in shaping a resilient and inclusive global economy.

Keywords: *Global Trade Dynamics, Emerging Markets, Export Opportunities and Trade Agreements*

Introduction

1. Agricultural Exports: Nourishing Growth and Prosperity

Agricultural exports play a pivotal role in driving economic growth and fostering prosperity for many countries. These exports involve the trading of agricultural products such as crops, livestock, and processed goods across international borders.This intricate web of trade not only nourishes nations but also nurtures opportunities for development, innovation, and sustainability. Let's delve into the myriad ways in which agricultural exports serve as a catalyst for growth and prosperity.

a) **Ensuring Food Security:** The role of agricultural exports in guaranteeing steady access to food, even in times of scarcity, cannot be overstated. For instance, amid the COVID-19 pandemic, these exports acted as a safeguard against food shortages across nations.

b) **Cultivating Income Streams:** By opening up avenues for farmers and producers to sell their goods abroad, agricultural exports become a means of generating income. This not only improves their own lives but also spurs investments within the agricultural sector.

c) **Sowing Job Opportunities:** The far-reaching impact of agricultural exports stretches beyond fields and farms, extending to the transportation, processing, and distribution sectors. The result is job creation that ripples through the economy.

d) **Fertilizing Economic Growth:** The demand surge triggered by agricultural exports initiates a growth cycle, stimulating economic expansion. This, in turn, fuels increased investment, leading to a self-sustaining growth trajectory.

e) **Cross-Border Trade Promotion:** The international exchange of agricultural products nurtures trade ties between nations. By dismantling trade barriers and improving economic efficiency, agricultural exports contribute to lowered prices and greater economic stability.

f) **Nurturing a Greener Earth:** The incentive of exports encourages farmers to embrace sustainable practices, championing environmentally friendly approaches such as efficient water use and reduced pesticide application.

g) **Catalyst for Developing Nations:** The transformative impact of agricultural exports on developing countries is profound. From reducing poverty and boosting food security to propelling economic development, these exports play a pivotal role.

h) **Glimpsing the Future:** With the global populace on the rise and income levels ascending, the demand for agricultural products is poised for exponential growth, presenting boundless opportunities for exporters

The fabric of global trade in 2020 saw agricultural exports constituting a remarkable 11% of merchandise trade. The foremost agricultural exporting giants encompass the United States, European Union, and China. The economic lifeline of many developing countries heavily relies on agricultural exports, with over half of their export revenues stemming from this sector. Unveiled by a comprehensive World Bank study, the ability of agricultural exports to slash poverty is a tangible reality, showcasing reductions of up to 10%.Undoubtedly, the safeguarding role of agricultural exports in a world beset by the COVID-19 pandemic showcased their indispensable role in averting food scarcity.

Section I: Evolving Patterns in Agricultural Exports

- **Surge in Emerging Market Influence:** The prominence of emerging markets is gaining momentum in the realm of agricultural trade. Their ascendancy is underpinned by factors like burgeoning populations, escalating incomes, and the swell of urbanization.
- **Rise in Processed Food Demand:** A mounting appetite for processed foods is sweeping through developing nations. Urbanization, altered dietary habits, and the soaring popularity of convenience foods are catalysts for this shift.
- **Thrust toward Organic and Sustainable Goods:** The call for organic and sustainable agricultural products is amplifying. Concerns about food safety, ecological impact, and animal welfare are driving this movement forward.
- **Accentuated Significance of Value-Added Offerings:** The call for value-added agricultural goods is echoing across the industry. Such products can command premium prices, elevating them above mere commodities.
- **Technology's Ascendant Role:** Technology is a lodestar in contemporary agricultural trade. Blockchain, big data, and artificial intelligence are spearheading enhanced traceability, transparency, and operational efficiency.

These trends hold profound implications for the future of agricultural trade, shaping its trajectory.

1. Illustrative Instances of Current Trends

- Emerging Market Momentum: China, the globe's most substantial agricultural importer, is swiftly augmenting its imports. Other burgeoning markets, notably India, Brazil, and Indonesia, are following suit.
- Processed Food Prowess: The processed food global market outpaces $1 trillion. Developing countries are leading this charge, registering robust growth in processed food demand.

- Organic and Sustainable Surge: The organic food market's valuation exceeds $100 billion globally. This movement is acutely pronounced in developed countries.
- Value-Added Vigor: The value-added agricultural products sector commands a substantial $500 billion worldwide. Developed nations exhibit a particular proclivity for these enhanced offerings.
- Tech-Driven Transformation: Technology's role is ascending swiftly in agricultural trade. Block chain tracks product movement, big data augments crop forecasts, and artificial intelligence spawns novel agricultural innovations.

In essence, the unfolding trends in agricultural exports reflect a dynamic landscape, driven by emerging market dynamics, shifting consumer preferences, and the relentless march of technology. As these trends continue to reshape the domain, the future of agricultural trade holds both promise and intrigue.

2. Global Demand Dynamics: A global surge in demand for agricultural exports is being fueled by several dynamic forces, reshaping trade dynamics.

Table 3: Key trends that are shaping the global demand dynamics of agricultural exports

Trend	**Description**
1. Population growth	The world's population is expected to grow to 9.7 billion by 2050, which will put a strain on the global food supply. This will lead to increased demand for agricultural exports, as countries seek to import food to meet the needs of their growing populations.
2. Changing diets	People are eating more meat and dairy products, which require more land and water to produce. In addition, people are eating more processed foods, which are often high in calories and low in nutrients. This shift in diets is also putting a strain on the global food supply and increasing demand for agricultural exports.
2. Economic development	As countries develop, people have more disposable income, which they can use to buy more food. This is especially true for meat and dairy products, which are seen as status symbols in many cultures. The increase in demand for these products is putting a strain on the global food supply, as well as on the environment.
3. Climate change	Climate change is affecting agricultural production in many parts of the world, leading to crop failures and food shortages. This is likely to increase demand for agricultural exports from countries that are less affected by climate change.
4. Trade policies	Trade policies can have a significant impact on the global demand for agricultural exports. For example, tariffs and other trade barriers can make it more expensive to import agricultural products, which can reduce demand.

Source: The United Nations Environment Program (UNEP)

2.1. Regions and Countries Driving the Demand

Asian region exhibits the highest demand across all three categories. Cereals are most in demand, with a substantial quantity of 508.1 million tons, reflecting the need to feed the continent's large population. Oilseeds and livestock products also hold significant importance, indicating the diverse dietary requirements and economic activities in the region. In Europe, cereals are still the most demanded agricultural category with 188.5 million tons, likely indicating their use for both human consumption and animal feed. Oilseeds and livestock products also play notable roles, illustrating the continent's reliance on these products for food and industry.

In North America Cereals are in demand, with 139.9 million tons, in line with the region's large population. Oilseeds and livestock products also contribute significantly to the region's agricultural trade, reflecting its consumption patterns and economic activities.Latin America region shows significant demand for cereals (107.7 million tons), possibly reflecting both domestic consumption and export. Oilseeds and livestock products are also important, reflecting the region's role as a major producer and exporter of agricultural commodities.

Cereals remain crucial in Africa, with 113.7 million tons demanded. This aligns with the continent's population and food security challenges. Demand for oilseeds and livestock products indicates the importance of these categories for local consumption and potential export. In Middle East and North Africa while cereals are in demand (79.1 million tons), the quantities are comparatively lower than in other regions, likely due to the region's arid climate and limited agricultural land. Oilseeds and livestock products also show notable demand, suggesting their significance for both local consumption and trade shown in table 4.

Table 4: The global agricultural products demand in 2022

Region	Top Categories Demanded Quantity (in million tons)		
	Cereals	Oilseeds	Livestock products
Asia	508.1	286.2	276.7
Europe	188.5	128.3	168.3
North America	139.9	112.4	122.8
Latin America	107.7	67.3	86
Africa	113.7	46.6	65.5
Middle East and North Africa	79.1	40.4	61.9

Source: ITC trade map

Table 5 shows that in China, the key agricultural demands revolve around cereals, oilseeds, and livestock products, bolstered by its status as the world's foremost producer and consumer of agricultural goods. Meanwhile, India's agricultural priorities encompass cereals, oilseeds, and pulses, aligning with its position as the second-largest global producer and consumer. The United States leads in demanding cereals, oilseeds, and livestock products, buoyed by its role as the planet's premier agricultural exporter. Brazil stands out for its demand for soybeans, corn, and beef, solidifying its stature as the largest exporter of soybeans and beef. Argentina's focus on soybeans, corn, and wheat secures its position as the world's fifth-largest soybeans exporter. Canada's requisites include wheat, canola, and livestock products, reflective of its prominence as the largest canola exporter. Australia, with its preferences for wheat, beef, and dairy products, ranks as the fourth-largest global wheat exporter. The European Union prioritizes cereals, dairy products, and meat, reaffirming its role as the world's foremost agricultural importer. Russia's appetite for wheat, corn, and sunflower oil aligns with its status as the largest wheat exporter. Finally, Indonesia's emphasis on rice, soybeans, and palm oil correlates with its distinction as the world's largest palm oil producer.

Table 5: Country wise largest demand of agricultural products

Country	Top Demanding Agricultural Products	Notable Status
China	Cereals, Oilseeds, Livestock	World's Largest Producer & Consumer
India	Cereals, Oilseeds, Pulses	World's 2nd Largest Producer & Consumer
United States	Cereals, Oilseeds, Livestock	World's Largest Agricultural Exporter
Brazil	Soybeans, Corn, Beef	World's Largest Soybeans & Beef Exporter
Argentina	Soybeans, Corn, Wheat	World's 5th Largest Soybeans Exporter
Canada	Wheat, Canola, Livestock	World's Largest Canola Exporter
Australia	Wheat, Beef, Dairy	World's 4th Largest Wheat Exporter
European Union	Cereals, Dairy Products, Meat	World's Largest Agricultural Importer
Russia	Wheat, Corn, Sunflower Oil	World's Largest Wheat Exporter
Indonesia	Rice, Soybeans, Palm Oil	World's Largest Palm Oil Producer

Source: ITC trade map

3. Analysis of How Different Countries Cater to Specific Market Preferences

This table showcases how various countries strategically align their agricultural production to cater to specific market preferences, leveraging their strengths and resources to optimize trade and contribute to global food security.

Table 6: Different countries cater to specific market preferences

Country	Specific Market Preferences	Key Agricultural Products	Strategy and Strengths
China	Rice, Wheat, Oilseeds, Pork, Vegetables	Rice, Wheat, Oilseeds, Pork, Vegetables	Meeting staple food needs, protein-rich diet, traditional preferences
Brazil	Soybeans, Coffee, Beef, Sugarcane	Soybeans, Coffee, Beef, Sugarcane	Leveraging arable land, climate advantage, biofuels industry
Italy	Wine, Olive Oil, Cheese	Wine, Olive Oil, Cheese	Emphasis on quality, tradition, and culinary heritage
Thailand	Rice	Rice	Tropical climate, staple food production, significant rice exports
Netherlands	Flowers, Dairy Products, Vegetables	Flowers, Dairy Products, Vegetables	Innovative greenhouse cultivation, advanced farming techniques
Australia	Wheat, Wool, Beef	Wheat, Wool, Beef	Abundant agricultural land, extensive grazing, global supply
India	Rice, Wheat, Spices, Pulses, Oilseeds	Rice, Wheat, Spices, Pulses, Oilseeds	Dietary diversity, protein-rich sources, traditional culinary elements
France	Wine, Cheese, Luxury Food Products	Wine, Cheese, Luxury Food Products	Quality, tradition, terroir, global culinary reputation
Argentina	Beef, Soybeans	Beef, Soybeans	Expansive grasslands, global protein and vegetable oil demand
Japan	Rice, Seafood	Rice, Seafood	Cultural preferences, island nation, focus on traditional staples
United States	Corn, Soybeans, Wheat	Corn, Soybeans, Wheat	Utilization of advanced technology, abundant land resources
Indonesia	Palm Oil, Rice, Rubber	Palm Oil, Rice, Rubber	Tropical climate advantage, global palm oil demand
New Zealand	Dairy Products, Meat	Dairy Products, Meat	Extensive pasturelands, high-quality production, global protein supply

Source: The International Food Policy Research Institute (IFPRI)

4. Trade Agreements and Market Access: India's trade agreements and market access for agricultural products:

a) **World Trade Organization (WTO):** India is a member of the WTO and participates in negotiations related to agriculture under the Agreement on Agriculture (AoA). This agreement aims to promote fair trade practices and reduce trade-distorting subsidies in agriculture.

b) **Regional Comprehensive Economic Partnership (RCEP):** India was initially part of negotiations for the RCEP, a regional trade agreement among ASEAN and its six FTA partners. However, India withdrew from the agreement in 2019 due to concerns about market access and protection of its domestic industries.

c) **India's Bilateral and Multilateral Trade Agreements:** India has various bilateral and regional trade agreements that impact its agricultural trade. Some of these agreements include Free Trade Agreements (FTAs) with countries like Sri Lanka, Thailand, and ASEAN nations. These agreements often involve tariff reductions and trade facilitation measures for agricultural products.

d) **Export Promotion Schemes:** India has implemented schemes like the Merchandise Exports from India Scheme (MEIS) to provide incentives to exporters, including those dealing with agricultural products. MEIS provides export incentives in the form of duty credits to promote exports of specific products.

e) **Phytosanitary and Sanitary Measures:** Agricultural trade involves adherence to phytosanitary and sanitary measures to ensure the safety of food and agricultural products. India's compliance with international standards, such as Codex Alimentarius, helps in gaining market access for its agricultural exports.

f) **Market Access Issues:** India has faced challenges in terms of market access for some of its agricultural products in various countries due to tariff barriers, non-tariff barriers, and sanitary and phytosanitary measures. Negotiations and bilateral discussions are often undertaken to address these issues.

g) **Agri-Export Zones and Quality Standards:** India has established Agri-Export Zones (AEZs) to promote the export of specific agricultural products by developing the entire supply chain. Additionally, adhering to quality standards like Good Agricultural Practices (GAP) and organic certifications enhances India's market access.

h) **Potential Future Agreements:** India continues to explore new trade agreements and partnerships to expand its agricultural exports. Negotiations with countries such as the United States, Australia, and the European Union have been discussed in the context of potential trade agreements.

Section II: Current Status of Agricultural Exports

1. Status of Exporting Countries in the World

The table 7 presents the agricultural export values (in billion U.S. dollars) of the top 10 countries over a span of five years, from 2018 to 2022. The United States consistently maintains the lead throughout these years, with its agricultural exports ranging from 144.3 billion dollars in 2018 to 154.8 billion dollars in 2022. Similarly, the European Union retains the second position, with exports gradually increasing from 136.2 billion dollars in 2018 to 142.4 billion dollars in 2022. China follows closely, experiencing a steady rise from 115.0 billion dollars in 2018 to 122.8 billion dollars in 2022. Brazil, ranked fourth, demonstrates consistent growth as well, with its exports escalating from 100.7 billion dollars in 2018 to 105.3 billion dollars in 2022. Argentina, India, Canada, Australia, Netherlands, and Thailand complete the list, each showcasing varying degrees of growth over the years. This data underscores the dynamism of global agricultural trade, as countries experience fluctuations in their export values influenced by factors such as economic conditions, demand fluctuations, and policy changes.

Table 7: 10 Agricultural Exporters in the World from 2018 to 2022 Value (USD Billion)

Rank	Country	2018	2019	2020	2021	2022
1	United States	144.3	145.4	144.7	154.5	154.8
2	European Union	136.2	137.2	138.3	142	142.4
3	China	115	117.3	118.2	122.5	122.8
4	Brazil	100.7	102	102.8	104.9	105.3
5	Argentina	53.8	54.6	55.1	56.3	56.5
6	India	49.3	50.6	51.3	52.9	53.2
7	Canada	43.7	44.3	44.7	45.7	46
8	Australia	39.6	40.2	40.5	41.3	41.5
9	Netherlands	38.2	38.7	39	39.7	39.9
10	Thailand	35.2	35.7	36	36.7	36.9

Source: Food and Agriculture Organization of the United Nations (FAO)

2. Top Exporting Products from India

Marine products emerge as the leading export category, consistently increasing in value from 12.8 billion dollars in 2018 to 14.7 billion dollars in 2022. Basmati rice, a sought-after variety of rice, follows with a steady growth trajectory, expanding from 8.8 billion dollars in 2018 to 9.8 billion dollars in 2022. Non-Basmati rice, another significant rice category, also experiences growth, with exports climbing from 7.6 billion dollars in 2018 to 8.5 billion dollars in 2022. Spices constitute another important category, with export values rising from 6.8 billion dollars in 2018 to 7.4 billion dollars in 2022. Buffalo meat, the fifth product in the ranking, displays a similar trend, with its exports reaching 4.8 billion dollars in 2022 from 4.4 billion dollars in 2018. Table presents the export values (in billion U.S. dollars) of specific agricultural products across a span of five years, from 2018 to 2022.

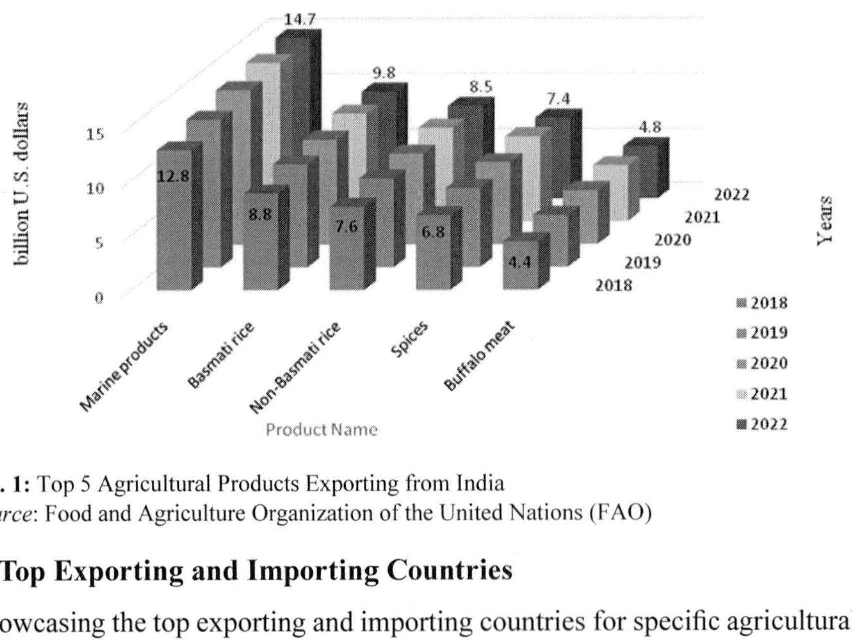

Fig. 1: Top 5 Agricultural Products Exporting from India
Source: Food and Agriculture Organization of the United Nations (FAO)

3. Top Exporting and Importing Countries

Showcasing the top exporting and importing countries for specific agricultural products in table 8, along with their corresponding export and import values in billion USD. The United States leads by exporting corn worth 27.1 billion USD to Mexico, while China exports soybeans valued at 26.7 billion USD to the Netherlands. Netherlands exports dairy products worth 9.3 billion USD to Germany, and Germany exports machinery and equipment valued at 8.9 billion USD to France. Brazil emerges as a significant exporter of soybeans, valued at 31.5 billion USD to China, which, in turn, imports meat worth 10.7

billion USD. France's wine exports amount to 6.9 billion USD to Italy, and Canada exports wheat valued at 12.6 billion USD to the United States, a major meat importer at 8.8 billion USD. Argentina also exports soybeans, 13.3 billion USD worth, to China, which continues to import meat, this time from Argentina, valued at 6.8 billion USD. Spain exports 6.8 billion USD worth of fruits and vegetables to Germany, a major machinery and equipment importer at 6.5 billion USD, and Belgium exports machinery and equipment worth 6.3 billion USD to the Netherlands, a significant food importer at 6.7 billion USD. Furthermore, India joins the spectrum by exporting Basmati rice worth 4.0 billion USD to the United Arab Emirates, while importing vegetable oils valued at 2.4 billion USD. This tableau underscores the intricate interplay of trade relationships across diverse agricultural categories.

Table 8: Top exporting and importing countries for agricultural products in the world, along with their corresponding values in million USD

Rank	Exporting Country	Importing Country	Top Agricultural Export Category	Export Value (in billion USD)	Top Agricultural Import Category	Import Value (in billion USD)
1	United States	Mexico	Corn	27.1	Vegetables	15.3
2	China	Netherlands	Soybeans	26.7	Meat	14
3	Netherlands	Germany	Dairy products	9.3	Machinery and equipment	10.2
4	Germany	France	Machinery and equipment	8.9	Meat	9.6
5	Brazil	China	Soybeans	31.5	Meat	10.7
6	France	Italy	Wine	6.9	Machinery and equipment	7.5
7	Canada	United States	Wheat	12.6	Meat	8.8
8	Argentina	China	Soybeans	13.3	Meat	6.8
9	Spain	Germany	Fruits and vegetables	6.8	Machinery and equipment	6.5
10	Belgium	Netherlands	Machinery and equipment	6.3	Food	6.7
11	India	United Arab Emirates	Basmati rice	4	Vegetable oils	2.4

Source: Food and Agriculture Organization of the United Nations (FAO)

3.1 Export-Import Status of India Country Wise

The provided table 9 illustrates India's agricultural trade relationships, highlighting its role as both an exporter and importer of various agricultural products, categorized by specific commodities. India, as the exporting country, leads the way by exporting spices valued at 3,328 million USD to the United Arab Emirates, and rice valued at 2,458 million USD to the United States. The import dynamics also come into play, where India imports dairy products worth 1,516 million USD in vegetable oils from the United Arab Emirates, and 1,251 million USD in dairy products from the United States. Among other notable trade relationships, India exports tea valued at 1,589 million USD to Sri Lanka, while importing fruits and vegetables worth 1,148 million USD, and jute and jute products worth 842 million USD from Saudi Arabia. The trade data underscores India's diversified role in the global agricultural trade market, where it engages in both export and import transactions for a range of essential agricultural commodities.

Table 9: Top agricultural exports and imports from India, along with their corresponding values in million USD

Rank	Exporting Country	Importing Country	Top Agricultural Export Category	Export Value (in million USD)	Top Agricultural Import Category	Import Value (in million USD)
1	India	United Arab Emirates	Spices	3,328	Vegetable oils	1,516
2		United States	Rice	2,458	Dairy products	1,251
3		Sri Lanka	Tea	1,589	Fruits and vegetables	1,148
4		Bangladesh	Jute and jute products	1,322	Cereals	1,023
5		Vietnam	Sugar	982	Coffee	431
6		Nepal	Spices	900	Cereals	385
7		Saudi Arabia	Jute and jute products	842	Fruits and vegetables	339
8		United Kingdom	Tea	782	Dairy products	306
9		Malaysia	Rice	755	Vegetable oils	298
10		China	Coffee	695	Spices	291

Source: Food and Agriculture Organization of the United Nations (FAO)

4. Quality and Safety Standards

Quality and safety standards play a pivotal role in trade relations between India and different countries. These standards ensure that agricultural products meet specific criteria to safeguard consumer health, maintain product integrity, and facilitate smooth cross-border trade. India adheres to international quality and safety norms, often regulated by organizations like the World Trade Organization (WTO) and the Codex Alimentarius Commission.

In its trade relations, India engages in the application of standards through various mechanisms, such as:

a) **Food Safety Regulations:** India enforces food safety regulations in line with international standards to ensure the safety of exported agricultural products. This includes adherence to regulations related to pesticides, contaminants, additives, and labeling, aligned with the Codex Alimentarius.

b) **Quality Certification:** Products are often required to undergo certification processes to verify their adherence to quality and safety standards. Certifications like ISO, HACCP (Hazard Analysis and Critical Control Points), and organic certifications assure importing countries of the products' quality and safety.

c) **Sanitary and Phytosanitary Measures (SPS):** India complies with SPS measures laid out by the WTO, ensuring that exported agricultural products are free from pests, diseases, and contaminants. This facilitates the prevention of potential risks to importing countries' ecosystems and consumers.

d) **Mutual Recognition Agreements (MRAs):** India negotiates MRAs with trading partners to mutually recognize each other's product testing and certification procedures, simplifying trade and reducing duplication of processes.

e) **Traceability Systems:** Implementation of traceability systems ensures that the origins and journey of products are well-documented, aiding in quality control and risk mitigation.

f) **Phytosanitary Certificates:** For agricultural products, India provides phytosanitary certificates, indicating that products meet the importing country's plant health requirements.

g) **Bilateral Agreements:** India establishes bilateral agreements with partner countries to harmonize standards and facilitate trade while addressing concerns about quality, safety, and product authenticity.

h) **Export Inspection Council (EIC):** The EIC in India certifies processed and value-added products for export. It ensures products adhere to the importing country's standards.

These quality and safety standards not only foster trust among trading partners but also enhance India's reputation as a reliable source of agricultural products. Adherence to international norms ensures that products from India meet global benchmarks, leading to sustainable and mutually beneficial trade relationships.

5. Discussion of Challenges and Opportunities in Complying with These Standards

Complying with quality and safety standards in international trade relations presents both challenges and opportunities for India's agricultural sector.

Challenges

a) **Infrastructure and Technology:** Ensuring compliance requires robust infrastructure and advanced technology for testing, processing, and packaging. Lack of modern infrastructure can hinder meeting stringent standards.

b) **Capacity Building:** Effective compliance demands skilled manpower and technical expertise. The training of professionals to understand and implement complex regulations is crucial.

c) **Cost Implications:** Adhering to standards often entails additional costs for upgraded technology, testing facilities, and quality control measures. Smaller farmers and producers may find it financially burdensome.

d) **Diverse Requirements:** Different countries have varying standards, making it challenging for Indian exporters to navigate and adapt to multiple sets of regulations.

e) **Data Management:** Maintaining accurate records for traceability and quality control can be a logistical challenge, particularly for small-scale producers.

f) **Changing Regulations:** Global standards evolve, and keeping up with these changes requires constant monitoring and adaptation.

Opportunities

a) **Market Access:** Complying with international standards enhances access to global markets, as countries prefer products that meet their quality and safety norms.

b) **Export Diversification:** Adhering to standards allows India to expand its export basket, including value-added and processed products, increasing revenue potential.

c) **Quality Enhancement:** Meeting global standards encourages Indian producers to adopt modern practices, improving the overall quality of domestic products.

d) **Brand Building:** Consistently adhering to high standards builds India's reputation as a reliable source of safe and quality agricultural products.

e) **Investment and Collaboration:** The need to meet standards spurs investments in infrastructure and technology. Collaborations with foreign partners for knowledge and technology transfer can strengthen the sector.

f) **Value Chain Integration:** Compliance necessitates a coordinated approach along the supply chain. This integration enhances product quality and minimizes risks.

g) **Sustainable Practices:** Meeting standards often involves adopting sustainable practices, promoting environmental conservation and resource efficiency.

Way Forward

To harness the opportunities and overcome challenges, India needs to focus on:

a) **Capacity Building:** Invest in training programs and skill development to ensure producers, processors, and regulators understand and implement standards effectively.

b) **Infrastructure Development:** Develop modern testing labs, processing units, and logistics facilities to ensure products meet international benchmarks.

c) **Government Support:** Provide incentives, subsidies, and policy support to encourage compliance among small-scale producers and exporters.

d) **Research and Innovation:** Support research to develop innovative solutions for compliance, traceability, and quality enhancement.

e) **Public-Private Partnerships:** Collaboration between government agencies, industry bodies, and private players can collectively address challenges and streamline compliance efforts.

By leveraging opportunities and addressing challenges, India can navigate the complex landscape of quality and safety standards, bolstering its position in the global agricultural trade market.

Section III: Prospects for Future Agricultural Exports

1. Agricultural Products Trending in Emerging Markets

The table 10 outlines the potential and growth rates of various categories within the global food industry, shedding light on significant trends and opportunities. Functional foods, which offer health benefits beyond basic nutrition, are projected to reach a substantial market value of $236.3 billion by 2027, with a steady compound annual growth rate (CAGR) of 7.2% from 2022 to 2027. Organic foods, driven by consumer demand for healthier and more sustainable choices, are on an impressive growth trajectory, expected to reach $351.8 billion by 2025, with a remarkable CAGR of 12.2% from 2020 to 2025. Plant-based foods, a response to environmental and health concerns, are set to hit $162.8 billion by 2026, growing at a CAGR of 10.4% from 2021 to 2026. Sustainable foods, emphasizing environmentally conscious production, anticipate reaching $884.5 billion by 2025, driven by a CAGR of 10.9% from 2020 to 2025.

Table 10: Potential of agricultural products trending in emerging markets

Sr. No.	Product Category	Potential	Last 5 Year Growth Rate
1	Functional foods	The global functional foods market is expected to reach $236.3 billion by 2027, growing at a CAGR of 7.2% from 2022 to 2027. The market was valued at $156.9 billion in 2021.	7.50%
2	Organic foods	The global organic food market is expected to reach $351.8 billion by 2025, growing at a CAGR of 12.2% from 2020 to 2025. The market was valued at $240.3 billion in 2020.	12.50%
3	Plant-based foods	The global plant-based foods market is expected to reach $162.8 billion by 2026, growing at a CAGR of 10.4% from 2021 to 2026. The market was valued at $87.4 billion in 2021.	10.80%
4	Sustainable foods	The global sustainable food market is expected to reach $884.5 billion by 2025, growing at a CAGR of 10.9% from 2020 to 2025. The market was valued at $484.2 billion in 2020.	12.10%
5	Innovative food technologies	The global innovative food technologies market is expected to reach $32.1 billion by 2025, growing at a CAGR of 12.5% from 2020 to 2025. The market was valued at $15.5 billion in 2020.	13.50%

Source: Grand View Research report 2022

Finally, innovative food technologies, encompassing advancements in food processing and preservation, expect to achieve $32.1 billion by 2025, boasting a notable CAGR of 12.5% from 2020 to 2025. The consistent growth rates in these sectors over the last five years underscore their resilience and their alignment with evolving consumer preferences for healthier, more sustainable, and technologically advanced food options.Here are some specific examples of how businesses are capitalizing on the growth opportunities in emerging markets for agricultural products:

i. **Nestle:** Nestle is a Swiss multinational food and drink company. The company has a strong presence in emerging markets, and it is investing heavily in agricultural research and development in these markets. Nestlé is also working with farmers in emerging markets to improve their productivity and efficiency.
ii. **Cargill:** Cargill is an American multinational food and agricultural company. The company has a long history of operating in emerging markets, and it is one of the largest exporters of agricultural products from these markets. Cargill is also investing in agricultural infrastructure in emerging markets, such as ports and storage facilities.
iii. **Syngenta:** Syngenta is a Swiss multinational agricultural company. The company develops and sells crop protection products and seeds. Syngenta has a strong presence in emerging markets, and it is investing in agricultural research and development in these markets. Syngenta is also working with farmers in emerging markets to improve their productivity and efficiency.

These are just a few examples of how businesses are capitalizing on the growth opportunities in emerging markets for agricultural products. The agricultural sector in emerging markets is a dynamic and growing sector with a lot of potential for businesses. Businesses that are able to understand the needs of these markets and adapt their products and services accordingly are likely to be successful.

2. Emerging Markets and Growth Opportunities

Emerging markets offer promising growth opportunities for agricultural products, driven by factors like population growth, rising incomes, changing consumption patterns, and increasing urbanization. These markets present a fertile ground for agricultural exporters to tap into new demand sources. Some of the key emerging markets and growth opportunities include:

a) **Asia-Pacific Region:** With its growing population and expanding middle class, countries in Asia, such as China, India, Indonesia, and Vietnam, are witnessing increased demand for a variety of agricultural products. Rising urbanization and dietary shifts towards protein-rich foods are creating opportunities for exports of meat, dairy, processed foods, and value-added products.

b) **Middle East and North Africa (MENA):** Water scarcity and limited arable land in this region drive substantial reliance on food imports. Countries like Saudi Arabia, UAE, and Egypt are significant importers of staples like wheat, rice, and pulses. There is potential for exporting high-quality fruits, vegetables, and processed foods.

c) **Sub-Saharan Africa:** As income levels rise and urbanization continues, African countries are experiencing changing dietary habits. Demand for meat, dairy, and processed foods is on the rise. Additionally, the continent's agricultural potential provides opportunities for exports of staple crops, cash crops, and value-added products.

d) **Latin America:** This region is a key exporter of commodities like soybeans, beef, and coffee. Growing demand for these products, along with processed foods, presents opportunities to expand trade relations and diversify agricultural exports.

e) **Eastern Europe:** Countries in this region are gradually becoming more affluent, leading to increased demand for higher-quality and diverse food products. This creates prospects for exporting meat, dairy, fruits, and processed foods.

f) **South-East Asia:** The burgeoning middle class in countries like Thailand, Malaysia, and Philippines is driving demand for imported food products. These markets present growth opportunities for a wide range of agricultural exports.

g) **Central Asia:** Some countries in this region are modernizing their agricultural practices and seeking imports to meet growing consumer demands. This opens doors for agricultural trade in grains, fruits, and vegetables.

h) **South America:** Beyond traditional commodities, countries like Brazil and Chile offer opportunities in exporting niche products like organic produce and specialty crops to cater to global demand for health-conscious and unique offerings.

i) **Oceania:** Countries like Australia and New Zealand are well-known for their high-quality dairy and meat products. Expanding trade networks can create avenues for their agricultural exports to reach new markets.

To leverage these growth opportunities, exporters should consider factors like cultural preferences, regulatory environments, infrastructure readiness, and logistics. Moreover, focusing on sustainable and environmentally friendly practices can resonate well with emerging markets' evolving consumer preferences. By identifying and capitalizing on these emerging markets, agricultural exporters can establish a stronger global presence and drive growth in the sector.

Conclusion

Agricultural exports are a cornerstone of global trade, ensuring food security, economic growth, and sustainability. They are vital for future global development, especially considering the dynamic trends in emerging markets, rising demand for processed and sustainable foods, and technological advancements. Key players in agricultural exports, such as the United States, the European Union, China, and Brazil, experience fluctuations influenced by various factors.

India's diverse role in global agricultural trade involves both exports and imports, with significant products like spices, rice, and marine products. The country actively navigates the trade landscape through various agreements and adherence to international standards.

Quality and safety standards are crucial, offering market access and export diversification opportunities. India must focus on capacity building, infrastructure development, and government support to excel in this landscape.

India and other agricultural exporters have promising opportunities in emerging markets, driven by changing consumer preferences and rising incomes. Businesses, like Nestle, Cargill, and Syngenta, are capitalizing on these prospects. To succeed, understanding local markets, regulatory environments, and sustainability is key. The future of agricultural trade holds potential and intrigue, shaped by evolving trends, technological advancements, and emerging markets.

References

Alam, F., &Myovella, G. (2016). Causality between agricultural exports and GDP and its implications for Tanzanian economy.

Bairak, R. I., & Hughes, D. W. (1996). Evaluating the impacts of agricultural exports on a regional economy. Journal of Agricultural and Applied Economics, 28(2), 393-407.

Berry, A. (2001). When do agricultural exports help the rural poor? A political-economy approach. Oxford Development Studies, 29(2), 125-144.

Chambers, W., & King, R. P. (2002). Changing agricultural markets: Industrialization and vertical coordination in the dry edible bean industry. Applied Economic Perspectives and Policy, 24(2), 495-511.

Dawson, P. J. (2005). Agricultural exports and economic growth in less developed countries. Agricultural economics, 33(2), 145-152.

Ferro, E., Otsuki, T., & Wilson, J. S. (2015). The effect of product standards on agricultural exports. Food Policy, 50, 68-79.

Grant, J. H., Arita, S., Emlinger, C., Johansson, R., &Xie, C. (2021). Agricultural exports and retaliatory trade actions: An empirical assessment of the 2018/2019 trade conflict. Applied Economic Perspectives and Policy, 43(2), 619-640.

Hallam, D., & Tropical and Horticultural Products Service Raw Materials. (2004). The market for non-traditional agricultural exports (Vol. 3). Rome: FAO.

Kachru, R. P. (2010). Agro-processing industries in India: Growth, status and prospects. Journal Indonesian Agroindustries, 13(2), 167-181.

Katiha, P. K., Chakraborty, C., & Chakraborty, I. (2003). Processed and Non-Processed Fish Exports: Trends, Status and Prospects of India in World Fish Trade. Indian Journal of Agricultural Economics, 58(3), 619.

Kumar, V. (2021). Trends and performance of India's Agricultural Trade in the midst of COVID-19 pandemic. Indian Journal of Agricultural Economics, 76(3), 352-370.

Mehrara, M., &Baghbanpour, J. (2016). The contribution of industry and agriculture exports to economic growth: the case of developing countries. World Scientific News, (46), 100-111.

Ohlan, R. (2013). Agricultural exports and the growth of agriculture in India. Agricultural Economics, January.

Pick, D. H., & Park, T. A. (1991). The competitive structure of US agricultural exports. American Journal of Agricultural Economics, 73(1), 133-141.

Rehman, T., & Khan, M. U. (2019). Early trends, current status and future prospects of farm mechanization in Asia. Agricultural Engineering International: CIGR Journal, 21(3), 76-87.

Roberts, I., Haseltine, C., &Maliyasena, A. (2009). Factors affecting Australian agricultural exports. Canberra: ABARE.

Seok, J. H., & Moon, H. (2021). Agricultural exports and agricultural economic growth in developed countries: Evidence from OECD countries. The Journal of International Trade & Economic Development, 30(7), 1004-1019.

Shepherd, B., & Wilson, N. L. (2013). Product standards and developing country agricultural exports: The case of the European Union. Food Policy, 42, 1-10.

Singh, K., &Sain, I. (2003). Prospects of agricultural exports of India: A composite index approach. Indian Journal of Agricultural Economics, 58(4), 781-799.

Stepanova, E. V. (2020, August). Strategic directions for the development of agricultural exports in the regions of the Russian Federation. In IOP Conference Series: Earth and Environmental Science (Vol. 548, No. 2, p. 022098). IOP Publishing.

Thomas, S., & Sheikh, W. (2010). Growth and composition of Indian agricultural exports during reform era. Abhinav Journal of Research in Commerce & Management, 1(6), 92-104.

Uremadu, S. O., &Onyele, K. O. (2016). The impact of selected agricultural exports on the growth of the domestic economy. Academia Journal of Agricultural Research, 4(5), 281-291.

2

Agri Exports
Current Trends and Prospects in Bihar

Shravanthi, A.R.

School of Agribusiness and Rural Management
Dr. Rajendra Prasad Central Agricultural University, Pusa, Bihar

Abstract

This chapter explores the current landscape and future potential of agricultural exports from Bihar, a state with significant agrarian strengths yet modest global trade participation. Despite contributing robustly to India's production of fruits, vegetables, rice, and livestock, Bihar's share in national exports remains below 1%. The chapter presents a comprehensive analysis of Bihar's agricultural export trends, identifying key commodities such as Shahi Litchi, Katarni Rice, Jardalu mangoes, and millets and highlights emerging opportunities through Geographical Indication (GI) tags and high-value crops. A SWOT analysis underscores Bihar's strategic advantages, such as fertile soil and agro-climatic diversity, alongside weaknesses like infrastructure deficits, low market integration and poor access to export logistics. The chapter further outlines key threats such as flood prone regions, poor irrigation infrastructure, and limited cold storage capacity, while also examining growth potential through investment in multimodal transport, agri-processing zones, and farmer training. Policy suggestions include the development of export policies financial incentives and SEZs to boost Bihar's export readiness. Overall, the chapter emphasizes the importance of targeted strategies to transform Bihar into a competitive agri-export hub benefiting smallholder farmers and enhancing rural livelihoods.

Keywords: *Bihar Economy, Geographical Indications, Export Infrastructure, Agri-Export Policy and SWOT Analysis*

Introduction

India's agriculture industry is the primary means of sustenance for its population. The nation is distinguished as one of the most significant producers of agricultural goods and food items on a global scale (IBEF, 2023). During the past six years, the agricultural sector in India has been expanding at a rate that is equivalent to an "average annual growth rate" of 4.6%. The growth rate in 2021-22 was 3.0 percent, which is a decrease from the growth rate of 3.3% in 2020-21. Additionally, throughout the course of the past several years, India has swiftly become the country that exports the most agricultural products. In the fiscal year 2020-21, India's exports of "agricultural and allied products" increased by 18 percent compared to the preceding accounting period. The value of agricultural exports reached a new all-time high of $50.2 billion during the fiscal year 2021-22 (Economic Survey 2022-23).

According to Indiastat data, the agricultural export has increased enormously from the last year as shown in the figure 1.

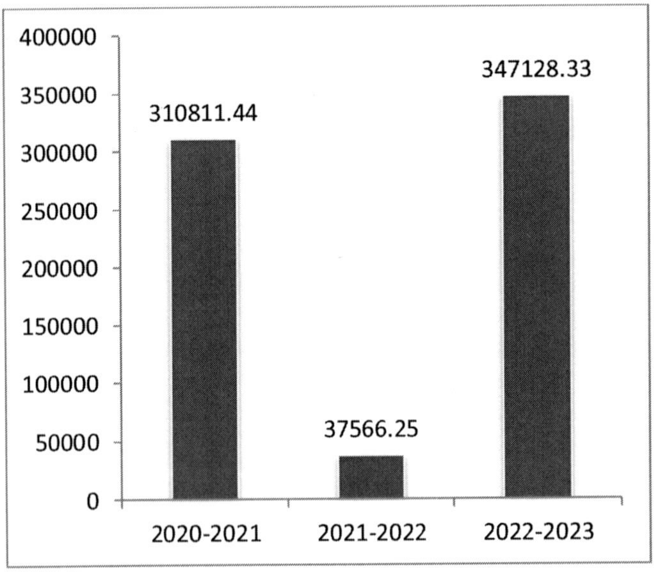

Fig. 1: Value of Total Agricultural Exports (in Crore Rupees) from 2020-21 to 2022-23

Table 1: Percentage Share of Agricultural Exports in National Exports

(Value in Crore Rs.)

Parameter	2020-2021	2021-2022	2022-2023
Total Agricultural Exports	310811.44	37566.25	347128.3
Total National Exports	2159043.22	2266092.22	2556900
Percentage Share of Agricultural Exports in National Exports	14.4	1.66	13.58

(Source: Indiastat data, 2023)

The percentage share of agricultural exports in national exports of our country is 13.58 for the year 2022-23.

Top five agricultural commodities that were exported from India in terms of quantity (in tonnes) for the year 2022-23 were marine products, spices, milled products and castor oil (Table 2). Whereas the top five commodities exported from India in terms of value (in crore rupees) for the year 2022-23 were marine products, regular rice, basmati rice, sugar and spices (Table 3).

Table 2: Top 10 Agricultural commodities exported from India (2022-23) in terms of quantity

(in tonnes)

S.No.	Commodities	Quantity
1	Marine Products	1443.41
2	Spices	1026.41
3	Milled Products	590.85
4	Castor Oil	523.55
5	Processed Fruits & Juices	514.48
6	Processed Vegetables	293.25
7	Coffee	250.15
8	Tobacco Unmanufactured	228.68
9	Tea	206.3
10	Sesame Seeds	193.91

(Source: Indiastat data, 2023)61

Table 2: Top 10 Agricultural commodities exported from India (2022-23) in terms of Value

S.No.	Commodities	Value
1	Marine Products	54961.11
2	Rice (Other than Basmati)	41272.89
3	Sugar	37397.86
4	Basmati Rice	30513.88
5	Spices	24195.98
6	Buffalo Meat	20967.01
7	Wheat	11728.36
8	Misc Processed Items	9054.99
9	Oil Meals	8941.49
10	Castor Oil	8366.06

(Source: Indiastat data, 2023)

Export Trends in Bihar

It is widely acknowledged that Bihar possesses a solid agricultural industry, which positions it as one of the most formidable agricultural states in the nationwide context. A far higher proportion of the population in Bihar is engaged in agricultural production than the national average—more than 80%.

Bihar is the third most productive state for vegetables and the fourth for fruits in the country.

Bihar is positioned at the 22nd rank nationwide in the export index, as per the report published by Niti Aayog on July 30, 2023. Based on the index, the Begusarai district has the biggest export volume in the state. Bihar is gradually progressing in terms of export growth across all dimensions. Currently, Bihar's share in the country's overall exports stands at a mere 0.52 percent. However, there are plans to raise this figure to 10 percent by the year 2025. Bihar is a prominent exporter of an extensive range of commodities, including but not limited to oil products, cattle, veggies, medicines, leather goods, baby corn, wheat, rice, maize and baby corn.

Other aspects of the export index are showing signs of progressive improvement and success for the state. The state of Bihar is ranked on the 27th spot in terms of its commercial ecology, the 13th spot in terms of its export policy, the 25th spot in terms of its export environment, the 29th spot in terms of its export performance, and the ninth spot in terms of exports among landlocked states.

It has been stated by Niti Aayog that the execution of the 'One District One Product' and 'Cluster Scheme' has resulted in an increase in the amount of goods that are exported from the state of Bihar. Additionally, there are intentions to sell goods from Bihar to 75 nations worldwide as part of the Amrut Mahotsav, which was organised to commemorate 75 years of Independence.

The state's agricultural exports are well-known to be growing. Bihar has exported agricultural commodities totaling Rs 26,71 crore by the end of 2021. From Muzaffarpur comes Shahi Litchi, while Bhagalpur is known for "Katarni Rice". Other products exported from the state include "Jardalu Mango", "wheat", "rice", "maize", "baby corn", vegetables and more.

Some of the agricultural goods that contribute to the overall exports of the nation are meat (which accounts for 6% of the total), rice (10%), wheat (1.3%), and fruits and vegetables (1.2%).

According to a report by APEDA (2022), millets are gaining popularity concurrently and about twenty one hundred metric tonnes of millets was exported from Bihar in the year 2021-22

SWOT Analysis on International Trade Prospects from Bihar

Strengths

- The three climate zones in Bihar are in the north-west, the north-east, and the south. Diversifying agriculture is possible in all three zones.

The state benefits from diverse agro-climatic zones, which provide a favourable environment for growing a wide range of profitable crops, vegetables, and fruits.

- Bihar possesses ample "natural resources", including "fertile soil" and "groundwater".
- Bihar is renowned for its robust agriculture sector, characterised by exceptionally high productivity.
- Bihar possesses Geographical Indications (GI) for numerous agricultural commodities. The UK received its first shipment of Shahi Litchi from Bihar in 2021, which was certified with a Geographical Indication (GI) label.
- The state benefits from its strategic geographical location, which provides it with advantages such as close proximity to the large markets of eastern and northern India, easy access to ports like Kolkata and Haldia, and availability of raw materials and mineral reserves from adjacent states.
- Bihar is renowned for its robust agricultural sector, making it one of the most formidable states in the country in terms of agriculture. In Bihar, almost 80% of the population is engaged in agricultural production, a significantly greater proportion than the national average.
- The state ranks fourth in vegetable production and eighth in fruit production in India.
- Industries related to food processing, dairy, sugar, healthcare, and manufacturing are experiencing rapid growth in the state.
- The state possesses a substantial pool of affordable industrial workforce, rendering it a very suitable location for a diverse array of enterprises.
- The cultivation of sugarcane occupies almost 6% of Bihar's total arable land. The state's sugarcane output during 2018–19 was 182.85 lakh metric tonnes. In the sugar season of 2019-20, there were a total of 11 operational "sugar mills" in the state of Bihar. Approximately 220.50 lakh metric tonnes of sugar were predicted to have been produced in Bihar over the 2019-20 year. The excess produce can be exported to other nations. Bihar's sugar exports amounted to US$ 6.41 million in FY22, up to February.
- Bihar presently possesses 68 industrial regions and mega industrial parks.

Weakness

- The high concentration of people living in rural areas, along with unpredictable fluctuations in rainfall, has led to increasing instability in agricultural growth and hindered efforts to diversify the agricultural sector.
- A lot of people in the state are still living in poverty. A farmer family in the state made an average of Rs. 7175 a month from 2015 to 2016, which is less than the national average of Rs. 8931, according to NABARD's 2018 report. This makes it look like the state's farming situation is not looking good.
- The "Agriculture Census" of 2015-16 says that small and poor farmers in Bihar own 96.9% of the land and grow crops on 75.9% of the land that is farmed.
- The large number of people living in rural places is the main reason why land is being broken up in the state.
- Earlier, we mentioned that although Bihar receives an adequate amount of rainfall for agriculture, there are uncertainty regarding the timing and distribution of rainfall. Consequently, agriculture in Bihar continues to rely significantly on irrigation.
- Insufficient productivity resulting from a lack of advanced technology. The country experiences the most minimal crop harvests and farmer incomes.
- Production is characterised by instability and often lacks high quality criteria for export.
- Challenges related to the handling, storage, packaging, and high expenses associated with post-harvesting processes.
- The after harvest processing in the state is inadequate.
- Insufficient market information systems in rural locations.
- Traders have a significant presence in Bihar. However, the absence of the APMC statute in the state means that there are no commission agents participating.
- There is a near-total lack of government acquisition of crops in Bihar. Consequently, farmers receive a price for their produce that is lower than the Minimum Support Price (MSP).
- Insufficient prior knowledge in navigating developed markets and export protocols.

- Farmers in Bihar have the lowest level of market engagement. One significant factor contributing to this is the limited size of farmers, resulting in a low production volume that only satisfies their own consumption needs. In fact, 98% of the farmers who didn't sell any of their crops said that they didn't because they were going to eat them themselves.
- During the "dry season" in Bihar, when the "water table" is still high, irrigation could potentially contribute to waterlogging, which would exceed any potential benefits that could be gained from practicing irrigation.
- One crucial factor that affects development is the presence of sufficient, dependable, and high-quality electricity at a reasonable price. However, the state consistently lacks in this aspect. The power intensity ratio, which measures the amount of energy consumed per hectare, highlights the remarkably low electricity consumption of the agricultural sector in Bihar. The inadequate condition of electricity supply for irrigation is a primary factor contributing to the underutilization of the state's aquifers that held lot of freshwater.
- Bihar made the distinct decision to revoke the "APMC Act" in 2006, and currently, there is no regulation governing "agricultural marketing" in place. In their report, Kishore et al. (2014) stressed that the period after the Agricultural Produce Market Committee (APMC) in Bihar has resulted in a varied experience for various parties involved. Following the restructuring of the Agricultural Produce Market Committee (APMC), the market environment has become more open, which benefits processing industries. They now have more options for acquiring agricultural produce without having to pay mandi taxes. Due to the early stage of development in the food processing business in Bihar, the benefits are now restricted.
- Despite progress in milk production, the state lacks genetically better animals needed for increased milk yield. Efforts to improve milk acquisition and processing in the state remain important.
- In terms of total meat production, mutton and pork take the lead, with buffalo and poultry following closely behind. The absence of contemporary "abattoirs" equipped with processing capabilities and efficient connections to both suppliers and distributors has hindered the expansion of value-added goods in this industry.
- Bihar has a lower road density compared to several other states. The proportion of paved roads in the overall road network is at 59.8%, which is below the average for the entire country.

- Insufficient marketing infrastructure has resulted in the FCI acquiring just a limited amount of food grains from Bihar.
- The poultry industry in Bihar is experiencing significant challenges due to the absence of contract farming.

Opportunities

- The state has devised strategic programmes to foster the growth of many sectors, including education and tourism. Additionally, it offers incentives to support projects related to information technology and renewable energy.
- "The Department for Promotion of Industry and Internal Trade" (DPIIT) reports that Bihar received a total of US$ 167.09 million in foreign direct investment (FDI) between October 2019 and December 2021.
- The state's total merchandise exports amounted to US$ 2,080.86 million in the period of 2021-22, namely till February 2022.
- Under the state budget for 2022-23, a sum of Rs. 8,365 Crore (US$ 1.09 billion) has been designated for infrastructure construction, specifically the creation of roadways and bridges. This investment aims to enhance the transportation infrastructure for agricultural goods, facilitating their movement from the state to nearby ports.
- In the state budget for 2022-23, a total of Rs. 7,712 crore (US$ 1 billion) was allocated specifically for agricultural and related activities. Hence, there is potential for an excess and enhanced agricultural output from the state in the foreseeable future. In February 2022, Mr Sarbananda Sonowal, the Minister of Port, Shipping and Waterways, initiated the construction of Bihar's inaugural multimodal inland waterways freight terminal at Kalughat near Sonepur in the Saran district. This development will enhance the efficiency of water transportation.
- In October 2020, "Mr. Ravi Shankar Prasad", the "Minister of Communications, Electronics & Information Technology", said that 46,000 villages in Bihar would be linked with an optical fibre network. This initiative aims to enhance connection and communication inside the state, particularly in rural areas.
- In March 2021, the state government declared its intention to offer electricity connections to all agricultural land in the state at a reduced rate. This initiative aims to resolve power-related challenges faced by farms, particularly in activities such as irrigation, intercultural operations, and post-harvest processing.

- In Bihar, as of April 2022, more than 100,000 farmers have received training in climate-resilient agricultural techniques since the commencement of a pilot project in 2019. The project was implemented in 40 villages across eight districts.
- The practice of growing a wide variety of fruits and vegetables in the state serves as a strong basis for "high-value agriculture" and the food processing business. Vegetable gardening shows great potential in Bihar. Bihar ranked fourth in vegetable production, following West Bengal, UP, and MP. The state of Bihar cultivates several vegetables including potato (which accounts for approximately 38% of the vegetable area), okra, brinjal, cabbage, cauliflower, onion and tomatoes. It is estimated that the productivity of fruit farming in Bihar is roughly 14.9 metric tonnes per hectare, which is somewhat higher than the national average of 14.6 metric tonnes per hectare. The primary fruits cultivated in Bihar include mango, banana, litchi, and guava. Bihar is the foremost state in litchi production in the country, contributing to around 42.7% of the total output. About 8.9% of the world's mangoes come from Bihar, making it the fifth biggest producer.
- In addition to agriculture, animal husbandry is a major economic driver in Bihar, creating jobs and wealth. Bihar possesses abundant livestock and poultry resources.
- Bihar encompasses a submerged area of 273.3 thousand hectares and has a river length of 3200 km. This confers a competitive edge to the state in terms of fish output.The State possesses robust weaving customs. The State has a weaver population over 90,000. The primary hubs for the textile industry in Bihar are Bhagalpur, Gaya, Nalanda, Darbhanga, Madhubani, Siwan, and Patna. Bihar is the second largest state in India in terms of jute production and jute textiles, following West Bengal. Some jute mills are situated in the northern portion of Bihar because to the presence of abundant raw jute, inexpensive labour, ample power, water, and transportation facilities in this area. Jute mills are situated at Karbisganj within the Purnia district, as well as in Katibar and Muktapur within the Samstipur district.Bihar possesses a significant proportion of the nation's goat and cattle population. Bihar is renowned for its superior cow hides, buff calf skins, and goat skins, owing to its abundant cattle population. The annual production amounts to 2.64 million bovine skins. The state possesses both tanneries and footwear factories in the private sector. Bihar state ranks third in the country for goats, following only West Bengal and Rajasthan. Consequently, the state offers significant opportunities for the leather tanning industry.

- Additional potential export sectors in Bihar include the processing of makhana, organic rice, honey, tea in Eastern Bihar, as well as aromatic oils such as mentha and lemon grass.

Threat

- In northern Bihar, over 76% of the population is at risk of flooding, while in southern Bihar, about 72% of the population is at risk of severe drought, according to the Water Resource Department.
- The state has consistently used more fertilisers per hectare than the national average throughout the last ten years. In the year 2015-16, the consumption of Bihar was approximately 201 kilogrammes per hectare, but the national average was 130.7 kilogrammes per hectare. According to the data from the Directorate of Economics and Statistics (DES), wheat farming in Bihar required 125 kg per hectare, while paddy required 97 kg per hectare in the year 2012-13. Concerns regarding the likelihood of subsidised fertilisers being supplied to surrounding nations are raised by the discrepancy in fertiliser usage numbers given by DES (Gulati 2016).
- In recent years, the total number of Kisan Credit Cards (KCCs) that Bihar's banks—scheduled commercial banks, regional rural banks, and central co-operative banks—have issued has decreased. Overall, 71.6% of banks were successful in fulfilling their targets in 2013–14; however, this figure fell to 35.5% in 2017–18. It is possible that the decreased performance in reaching the 2017–18 aim was caused in part by the lack of up-to-date applicant records. As a consequence of the land ownership statute, which acts as collateral for the acquisition of institutional credit, there has been a gradual increase of agricultural lending for scheduled commercial banks, regional rural banks, and central co-operative banks. This is because there is a shortage of current land records. Nevertheless, the state is fully aware of the situation and is actively taking steps to modernise its records. Once advancements are achieved in this area, farmers will have the opportunity to obtain additional agricultural finance for activities such as mechanisation and the growth of crop and livestock farming.
- The primary focus of crop insurance is to offer assistance to the agricultural industry. The Pradhan Mantri Fasal Bima Yojana (PMFBY) was introduced in India in 2016. Bihar created its own agricultural insurance scheme, known as the Bihar State Crop Assistance Programme (Bihar Rajya Fasal Sahayata Yojana), in response to its discontent with

the implementation of the Pradhan Mantri Fasal Bima Yojana (PMFBY). According to the Pradhan Mantri Fasal Bima Yojana, the national and state governments each contributed 49% of the premium amount, while the farmer's contribution was only 2% of the premium amount. Farmers who have registered under the state's agricultural support system are not required to pay any premium. Nevertheless, farmers are entitled to receive remuneration in case of agricultural losses resulting from natural disasters. As per this initiative, the state government would provide financial assistance of Rs. 7500 per hectare to farmers who are registered, for a maximum of two hectares, if their crop yield falls below 20% of a predetermined production limit (Vajpayee 2018). This approach will necessitate a higher fiscal burden on the state government, as a substantial portion of the monies designated for the agricultural sector may have to be reallocated towards this programme.

- Water availability fluctuations have had an impact on agriculture in Bihar. The state government has mostly employed the construction of embankments as the key technique to mitigate flood damage. However, these embankments can also pose a concern since the lands beyond the embankments are deprived of the valuable alluvial deposits that the river carries. Additionally, there is a potential danger of embankment breaches, which can cause significant disruption for communities living in proximity to embankments. Bihar contributes approximately 8.4% of the overall vegetable production in the country and about 4.8% of the fruit production. However, Bihar only has four percent of the total cold storage facilities in India.

Agri- Export Prospects in Bihar

- Onions, tomatoes, potatoes, brinjal, and rice are among the many vegetables and fruits grown for export, along with bananas, mangoes, and litchi.
- Bihar is rich in several locally available agricultural products which are known for their quality and distinctiveness. These agricultural products often have GI tags or have the potential to be proposed for GI tags. In an effort to encourage the export of agricultural products that are obtained locally and are tagged with Geographical Indications (GI), the National Bank for Agriculture and Rural Development (NABARD) in the state of Bihar has identified six prospective products that might be registered for a GI tag through the process of registering them. As per the GI registry portal, Bihar has 15 items and logos that have been granted the GI tag. Among the varieties available are Shahi Litchi,

Bhagalpuri Zardalu mango, Katarni rice, and Magahi Paan (betel leaf). The renowned makhana, also known as the fox nut, was officially awarded a Geographical Indication (GI) tag in December 2021.

Agri- Export Challenges in Bihar

Despite the significant potential for agricultural exports from Bihar, the current results do not match expectations due to many factors. Some of them include:

- The lack of built infrastructure for exports in the state is a well-established fact. Currently, there is no existing Special Economic Zone (SEZ) in the state, which means that exporters are unable to utilise custom clearing services.
- Despite possessing a geographical indication (GI) tag, numerous products from Bihar are encountering hindrances in their export due to the lack of an export policy.
- Power deficits are common issues in Bihar. To improve their export business ecosystem, Bihar should focus on improving power supply (Niti Aayog, 2022).
- Ensuring connectivity between landlocked production areas like Bihar and ports or terminals poses a significant problem. Furthermore, the infrastructure of the link roads that connect farms to the main road is insufficient in Bihar (Yes bank report).
- Currently, there is no provision for providing financial assistance for transporting items to ports or airports for export. However, multiple government authorities have expressed their willingness to support exporters from the state.

Suggestions to improve export from Bihar

Based on the recommendations derived from a research conducted by the Exim Bank, the suggestions to improve exports from Bihar include:

- Enhance the infrastructure for monitoring product quality in accordance with international market standards.
- Provide monetary incentives to exporters and implement advertising campaigns to promote exports.
- Establishing a customs clearing office within the existing inland container depot in Patna, as well as constructing inland container depots (ICDs) in Muzaffarpur and Bhagalpur, are both recommended. In addition, be certain that the necessary certificates must be obtained in order to fulfil export requirements.

- It is recommended that the establishment of exclusive economic zones be carried out in Patna, Muzaffarpur, and Bhagalpur, along with the enhancement of the infrastructure for cold chain and warehousing operations throughout the entire state.
- Without infrastructure, exporters face higher costs. To mitigate this issue, provide subsidies for freight prices. If exporters incur additional expenses as a result of governmental policy, they should be reimbursed.

Conclusion

Exports play a crucial role in stimulating economic growth by enabling a country to expand its reach beyond domestic markets and into larger markets, so gaining access to new opportunities. The exposure of enterprises to global markets incentivizes them to strive for greater productivity and efficiency in order to enhance their competitiveness. The revenue earned from exports can be utilized to invest in research, enhance production capabilities, develop employment opportunities, and fortify infrastructure within a nation. Therefore, exports play a crucial role in the development of a country by enhancing its total economic performance. India has been utilizing its trade policies to exploit the growth potential of exports in order to promote development within the country. Bihar possesses significant potential for agricultural exports, considering its impressive production statistics for many agricultural and related commodities. Nevertheless, there are specific obstacles to enhancing agricultural exports from the state. The state should prioritise addressing these obstacles by formulating policies that promote agricultural exports from Bihar. This approach will not only enhance the state's revenue, but also benefit the small-scale farmers and all other parties engaged in the agricultural supply chain.

References

Agriculture and Food Management: From Food Security to Nutritional Security (Chapter 8) (2023). Economic Survey 2022-23. Department of Economic Affairs, GOI. Retrieved from https://www.indiabudget.gov.in/economicsurvey/?q=agriculture

Agriculture Census. (2015–16). All India report on number and area of operational holdings. Retrieved May 2019, from Agricultural Census: http://agcensus.nic.in/document/agcen1516/T1_ ac_2015_16.pdf.

Agriculture in India: Agricultural Exports & Food Industry in India | IBEF. (2023, August). India Brand Equity Foundation. Retrieved from https://www.ibef.org/exports/agriculture-and-food-industry-india

Agro and Food Processing: Project Opportunities in Bihar. Retrieved from https://www.entrepreneurindia.co/project-and-profile-listing?CatId=138&SubCatId=135&CatName=Best%20Business% 20Opportunities% 20in%20 Bihar%20 -% 20Identification% 20and%20Selection%20of%20right%20Project,%20

Thrust%20areas%20for%20Investment,%20Industry%20Startup%20and%20Entrepreneurship&Page=5

APEDA. (2022). E - Catalogue For Export of Millets And Value Added Products Bihar. Retrieved from https://apeda.gov.in/milletportal/files/Bihar_Millet_Value_Added_Products_Catalogue.pdf

Chatterjee S., Krishnamurthy, M., Kapur, D. and Bouton, M. 2020. A Study of the Agricultural Markets of Bihar, Odisha and Punjab. Final Report. Center for the Advanced Study of India, University of Pennsylvania: Philadelphia.

Export Preparedness Index. (2022). Niti aayog. Retrieved from https://www.niti.gov.in/sites/default/files/2023-07/Export-Preparedness-Index-2022_0.pdf

Gulati, A. (2016). From plate to plough: Twenty-five years of tinkering. Indian Express, July 4, 2016. http://indianexpress.com/article/opinion/columns/india-economic-reformsindian-farmersfertiliser-subsidy-union-budget-modi-govt-organic-farming-2892089/.

Hoda, A., Gulati, A., Jose, S., Rajkhowa, P. (2021). Sources and Drivers of Agricultural Growth in Bihar. In: Gulati, A., Roy, R., Saini, S. (eds) Revitalizing Indian Agriculture and Boosting Farmer Incomes. India Studies in Business and Economics. Springer, Singapore. https://doi.org/10.1007/978-981-15-9335-2_8

https://agriexchange.apeda.gov.in/news/NewsSearch.aspx?newsid=43635

https://www.ibef.org/states/bihar

https://www.investindia.gov.in/state/bihar

Indian Agri Exports: Study on Difficulties faced by the exporters in the supply chain of agriculture products. Report by YES institute and APEDA. Retrieved from https://apeda.gov.in/apedawebsite/Announcements/APEDA_REPORT_22_Sep_16.pdf

Kishore, A., Sharma, B., & Joshi, P. K. (2014). Putting agriculture on the takeoff trajectory: Nurturing the seeds of growth in Bihar, India. New Delhi, India: International Food Policy Research Institute (IFPRI) and International Water Management Institute (IWMI).

Market News. APEDA. Retrieved from

NABARD. (2018). NABARD All India Rural Financial Inclusion Survey 2016–17. Mumbai: NABARD

Promoting exports from Bihar: Insights and Policy perspectives. (2019). Export-Import Bank of India. Retrieved from https://www.eximbankindia.in/Assets/pdf/research-on-states/Bihar.pdf

Swaroop, V. (2022, June 20). To promote exports, Bihar identifies six local products for GI tag | Latest News India. Hindustan Times. Retrieved from https://www.hindustantimes.com/india-news/to-promote-exports-bihar-identifies-six-local-products-for-gi-tag-101655735565317.html

3

Export Performance of Fresh Grapes from India

Mohit Kumar, Vipul S.G. and Ganga Devi

Department of Agricultural Economics, B.A. College of Agriculture
Anand Agricultural University, Anand, Gujarat, India

Abstract

India, recognized as leading producer of fruits, holds a significant position in global grape cultivation. This chapter comprehensively examines the export performance of fresh grapes from India, focusing on growth patterns, market diversification, competitiveness, and trade direction. During 2019-20, India exported over 193 thousand metric tons of grapes worth Rs. 2,176.88 crores, with the Netherlands, Russia, and the UK being key markets. Using compound annual growth rate (CAGR) analysis, the study finds significant positive trends in grape exports across major destinations. Instability indices reveal moderate fluctuations, with Bangladesh and Hong Kong showing the highest volatility, whereas the UAE demonstrated market stability. The decreasing trend in the Hirschman index indicates growing diversification in India's grape exports. Comparative advantage analysis (RSCA) suggests India gained competitiveness post-2015. Nominal Protection Coefficient (NPC) values below unity further underscore India's export price advantage. Mark Chain analysis reveals stable future prospects, with Netherlands projected to remain India's top grape importer through 2022-23. The findings provide strategic insights for exporters and policymakers to strengthen India's position in global grape markets by aligning trade efforts with loyal importers and emerging high-value destinations.

Keywords: *Fresh Grapes Exports, Instability Index, Geographical Concentration Index, Export Competitiveness and Markov Chain Analysis*

Introduction

Exports play a crucial role in fortifying a nation's economy, constituting a significant portion of its total national income. The impact of exports extends beyond mere numbers, as they not only create employment opportunities for the citizens but also amplify the global market presence of domestic products, thereby unlocking fresh prospects for trade and commerce. When a country ventures into the international market, it gains access to an extensive consumer base, which becomes instrumental in nurturing economic growth and fostering prosperity.

In the year 2018, India observed a remarkable export performance with goods and services measuring an impressive $322.29 billion USD, contributing to a significant 19.74 per cent of its GDP. However, the country's imports surpassed this figure, constituting a higher share of 23.64 per cent of its GDP, leading to India being classified as a net trade deficit nation. Unfortunately, India's trade growth rate for that specific year was a mere 0.87 per cent, notably lower than the global trade growth rate of 3.50 (World Bank , 2020). These figures underscore the challenges that India encountered in achieving a more balanced and resilient trade landscape.

India has established itself as a noteworthy exporter, offering an extensive range of approximately 7,500 diverse commodities to a vast network of 190 countries. However, despite its robust export activity, India's share in the global export market remains relatively modest, amounting to only 1.7 per cent of the world's total exports (International Trade Centre, 2019).

India has earned widespread recognition as a global hub for cultivating a diverse array of fruits and vegetables, earning it the well-deserved title of "the fruits and vegetable basket of the world". The country takes pride in its vast abundance of fruit and vegetable varieties, making it an ideal location for their cultivation. In the realm of fruit production, India proudly holds the second-largest position globally, closely trailing behind China. Furthermore, India stands at the forefront as the leading producer of mangoes, bananas, papayas, and lemon and lime, adding to its distinctive and prominent role in fruit and vegetable production on the global stage.

Scenario of Fruits in the World

In the year 2019, fruit crops were cultivated over a substantial area of 65.29 million hectares worldwide, marking a noteworthy increase from 53.52 million hectares in the year 2000. Amongst the total fruit crop production area, grapes stand out as the most extensively cultivated fruit globally, covering an expansive 6.93 million hectares. China takes the lead in both the area and production of fruit crops. As the second-largest player in this domain, India secures the second position, boasting a share of 10.82 per cent in the total fruit crop area and 11.79 per cent in production (FAOSTAT, 2020).

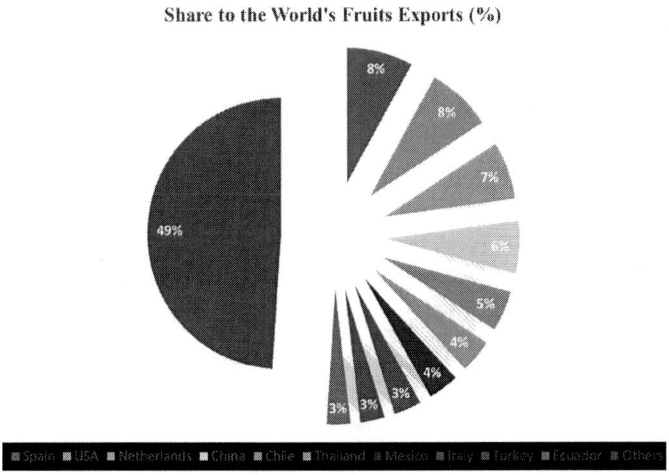

Fig. 1: Country-wise percentage share to world's total fruits exports

The global value of fruit exports amounts to $126.50 billion USD (FAOSTAT, 2020) provides the value of exports for major exporting countries along with their respective shares in the world's total fruit exports. Surprisingly, despite being the second-largest producer of fruits, India holds the 32nd position when it comes to the value of fruit exports. This discrepancy can be attributed to the substantial domestic demand within India's market, which likely reduces the quantity available for export.

In the broader context of overall fruit exports, bananas, grapes, and apples play a significant role, contributing with respective shares of 10.69 per cent, 7.07 per cent and 5.76 per cent (FAOSTAT, 2020). These fruits are among the leading commodities that find their way into the global market and showcase their popularity and demand worldwide.

Scenario of Fruits in India

The horticulture sector plays a crucial role in the Indian agriculture landscape, with the value of horticultural output contributing a significant 36.2 per cent to the overall agricultural output. Among the various horticultural crops, fruit crops hold a notable share of 31.4 per cent. India distinguishes itself as one of the few countries globally that cultivates a wide range of tropical, sub-tropical and temperate fruits. This advantage can be attributed to the diverse soil and climatic conditions present in the country, which allow for the cultivation of a rich variety of fruits.

In terms of land utilization, fruit production in India occupies approximately 2.36 per cent of the gross cropped area based on data from the year 2015-16 (Directorate of Economics and Statistics, 2020). This figure showcases the significance of fruit cultivation in the country's agricultural practices and reflects the nation's emphasis on this vital sector. During the fiscal year 2017-18, India's total agricultural exports amounted to □251,563.94 crore. Among these exports, the contribution of fresh fruits accounted for □4,913.28 crore, representing approximately 1.95 per cent of the total agricultural exports (Directorate of Economics and Statistics, 2020). It is notable that India's share in the global fruits and vegetables exports stood at a mere 1.4 per cent (Ministry of Finance, 2021). Conversely, in terms of imports, India acquired fresh fruits worth Rs. 12.52 thousand crore during the same period (Directorate of Economics and Statistics, 2020). These figures underscore the dynamics of India's trade in fresh fruits, showcasing both its export capabilities and its dependence on imports for meeting domestic demand.

Importance of Grapes

Grapes (Vitis vinifera) exhibit versatility in their cultivation, thriving in various climate zones, ranging from temperate to tropical regions. However, they particularly flourish in hot and dry climates, which are highly favorable for their growth. Notably, China has emerged as the leading global producer of grapes, boasting an impressive production volume of 14.28 million tons. In comparison, India secured the seventh position among the world's grape producers (FAOSTAT, 2020).

Within India, the area allocated for grape cultivation has witnessed a remarkable expansion, growing from 32.4 thousand hectares in 1991-92 to 138.9 thousand hectares in 2017-18. This significant increase in cultivated land reflects the country's growing interest and investment in grape production. Additionally, during the year 2017-18, grapes showcased an impressive productivity rate of 21 metric tons per hectare (Directorate of Economics and Statistics, 2020). These statistics vividly demonstrate the notable growth and productivity achieved by the grape industry in India over the years, solidifying its position as a significant player in the global grape market.

India primarily exports several grape varieties, including Thompson Seedless, Sonaka, Sharad Seedless, and Tas-e-Ganesh. Among these varieties, Thompson Seedless holds the highest share in terms of export volume. These grapes are sought after in international markets for their quality and taste.

In India, the peak harvesting season for grapes varies across different regions. In Maharashtra, which is the major grape-producing state, the peak harvesting period occurs from March to May. Karnataka, another significant grape-producing state, experiences peak harvesting in March, April and November. In Tamil Nadu, grape harvesting peaks in May and November. These timeframes represent the optimal periods for grape harvesting and export, ensuring that the grapes are fresh and of high quality for international markets.

Overall, the strategic timing of grape harvesting in different regions allows India to meet the demand for grapes in the global market and establish itself as a significant player in the international grape trade. The Agricultural and Processed Food Products Export Development Authority (APEDA) plays a crucial role in promoting and facilitating the export of Indian grapes to various countries.

Notably, Maharashtra's grape cultivation is concentrated in several key districts, including Nashik, Sangli, Solapur, Pune and Osmanabad, which have become prominent grape-producing regions. In Karnataka, the major grape-producing districts include Bijapur, Chikballapur, Belgaum, Bagalkot and Bangalore rural, contributing significantly to the state's grape output.

These statistics provide valuable insights into the substantial contribution of grape cultivation within India and highlight the regional distribution of this important agricultural activity. Maharashtra's leading position in grape production emphasizes its vital role in India's overall grape industry.

In the global market, an impressive quantity of 5.25 million metric tons of grapes, valued at 11.15 billion USD, was exported. The leading grape-exporting nations were Chile, Peru, the USA, South Africa and Turkey, with Chile holding the dominant position and contributing 17.54 per cent to the total value of grape exports. Peru closely followed with a share of 10.80 per cent.

In terms of grape exports, India secured the ninth position accounting for 3.84 per cent of the overall global grape exports in 2019 (FAOSTAT, 2020). While India's presence in the international grape export market is notable, it holds a relatively smaller share compared to the top grape-exporting nations.

These figures emphasize the significant role played by key grape-exporting nations in the global market and highlight India's position as a player in the international grape trade. While India is among the significant exporters, it faces competition from countries with larger shares in the global grape export market.

During the fiscal year 2019-20, India's grape export sector made significant strides, achieving a remarkable shipment of 193.69 thousand metric tons of grapes to international markets. This impressive export volume translated to a substantial value of Rs. 2176.88 crores. Among the various destinations for Indian grapes, the Netherlands, Russia, the United Kingdom, Bangladesh, and Germany emerged as major markets, demonstrating the global appeal of Indian grapes.

Notably, the Netherlands stood out as the top destination for Indian grapes, contributing a significant 36.13 per cent to the overall value of grapes exported from India during the 2019-20 period (APEDA, 2020). This highlights the growing prominence of India's grape exports and underscores the importance of key international markets in supporting the growth and development of the country's grape industry. These impressive statistics reflect the successful efforts made by India to expand its presence in the global grape market and establish itself as a notable player. The increasing demand for Indian grapes in these international markets showcases the quality and appeal of Indian produce on the global stage. It also signifies the industry's potential for further growth and continued success in meeting international demand.

Despite being the second largest fruit producer globally, India has not attained a leading position among fruit-exporting nations. The export of fresh fruits is a complex domain that necessitates a comprehensive analysis to understand the current landscape and guide future policy decisions. Consequently, this chapter aims to investigate the trade patterns of fresh grapes exports from India. Through this chapter, we seek to gain valuable insights into the dynamics of India's fresh fruit trade, which can aid in shaping effective strategies and policies for the future.

This chapter sheds light into various aspects of fresh grapes exports, including their growth patterns, instability, comparative advantage, and competitiveness within the overall export landscape of the country. By analyzing the export performance from a broader perspective, this research endeavors to identify changes in the direction of trade for specific fruit crops, which can provide insights into potential loyal import markets. The findings of this chapter are expected to offer valuable guidance to farmers, exporters, and policymakers in making informed decisions regarding crop selection, choosing export destinations, and implementing necessary policy changes. With these perspective in mind, the chapter entitled **"Export Performance of Fresh Grapes from India"** was undertaken.

Growth Rate of Exports

Growth Rate of Grapes Exports from India

The export of grapes from India to key destinations in the year 2019-20, along with their respective shares of the total exports, is outlined in Table 1. Notably, the Netherlands emerged as the largest importer of Indian grapes in both quantity and value terms, having imported a substantial 56.26 thousand metric tons of grapes valued at Rs. 786.72 crore during the aforementioned period. This indicates the significant demand and market presence of Indian grapes in the Netherlands.

The Netherlands made a substantial contribution to India's grape exports, accounting for 29.04 per cent of the total quantity and 36.14 per cent of the total value of grape exports during the year under review. In terms of export quantity, Bangladesh emerged as the second largest importer, having imported 32.74 thousand metric tons of grapes, representing a 16.9 per cent share of the total quantity exported. However, in terms of export value, Bangladesh had a relatively smaller share of 6.33 per cent. Despite importing a significant quantity of grapes, the value of these exports was comparatively lower

Indeed, in the fiscal year 2019-20, among the major destinations for Indian grape exports, Bangladesh had the lowest unit value of Rs. 4,209.98 per quintal. This indicates that the average value per quantity of grapes exported to Bangladesh was relatively lower compared to other destinations, reflecting different market dynamics and preferences in Bangladesh.

On the other hand, Russia stood out as the second-largest importer of Indian grapes, with imports valued at 265.58 crores. Russia's share accounted for 12.25 per cent of the total quantity of grape exports and 12.20 per cent of the total value, highlighting its significance as a crucial market for Indian grapes. The substantial value of grape exports to Russia indicates the country's demand for Indian grapes and showcases the opportunities for Indian exporters in the Russian market.

Among the major destinations, Hong Kong demonstrated the highest unit value of exports at Rs. 18,521.50 per quintal followed by Thailand with a unit value of Rs. 16,487.05 per quintal. This indicates that the average value per quantity of grapes exported to Hong Kong and Thailand was comparatively higher compared to other major destinations. This higher unit value signifies the preference for premium Indian grapes in these markets and the potential for Indian exporters to target and cater to the demand for high-quality grapes in these regions.

Table 1: Destination wise exports of grapes from India during the year 2019-20

Sl.No.	Country	Quantity ('000 MT)	Value (Crore `)	Unit Value (`/q)
1	Netherland	56.26 (29.04)	786.72 (36.14)	13,982.33
2	Russia	23.73 (12.25)	265.58 (12.20)	11,189.02
3	U K	14.48 (7.47)	205.44 (9.43)	14,183.74
4	Bangladesh	32.74 (16.90)	137.84 (6.33)	4,209.98
5	Germany	8.71 (4.50)	136.69 (6.27)	15,677.39
6	UAE	12.12 (6.26)	112.35 (5.16)	9,263.70
7	Saudi Arabia	8.70 (4.49)	77.29 (3.55)	8,875.14
8	Thailand	3.56 (1.84)	58.85 (2.70)	16,487.05
9	Hong Kong	2.38 (1.22)	44.10 (2.02)	18,521.50
10	Malaysia	2.67 (1.38)	38.32 (1.76)	14,338.17
11	Others	28.28 (14.60)	313.63 (14.40)	11,090.27
12	Total	193.69 (100)	2176.86 (100)	11,238.90

Source: FAOSTAT (2020) Figures in the parenthesis are percentage share to the total exports

Table 2 provides the destination-wise growth rates of grape exports to major importing countries and other destinations. The analysis reveals that exports of grapes to all major destinations, as well as other destinations, demonstrated positive growth rates. These growth rates were found to be statistically significant in terms of quantity, value, and unit value of the commodity during the study period. This indicates a consistent and substantial increase in grape exports to various destinations, highlighting the overall positive performance of the grape export market.

The analysis of quantity-based growth rates for grape exports to various destinations revealed interesting findings. Russia exhibited the highest annual growth rate of 35.6 per cent, which was statistically significant at the 1 per cent level. Thailand also displayed a remarkable growth rate of 33.47 per cent per annum, which was also significant at the 1 per cent level. Noteworthy growth rates were also observed in the quantity of grape exports to Netherland (20.29%), Hong Kong (25.80%), and Saudi Arabia (22.52%). On the other hand, the United Kingdom showed the lowest growth rate of 5.04 per cent per annum, followed by the United Arab Emirates (5.86%), both of which were significant at the 1 per cent level.

Table 2: Country wise compound annual growth rates (%) of India's grapes exports (2000-01 to 2019-20)

Sl. No.	Country	Quantity	Value	Unit Value
1	Netherland	20.29** (0.481)	27.31** (0.417)	5.83** (0.164)
2	Russia #	35.60** (0.690)	39.60** (0.665)	2.26** (0.069)
3	U K	5.04** (0.292)	12.17** (0.306)	6.79** (0.137)
4	Bangladesh	16.15* (1.386)	26.20** (1.250)	8.65** (0.331)
5	Germany	16.06** (0.828)	25.91** (0.802)	8.48** (0.302)
6	UAE	5.86** (0.167)	12.15** (0.164)	5.94** (0.169)
7	Saudi Arabia	22.52** (0.609)	29.73** (0.466)	5.89** (0.213)
8	Thailand ##	33.47** (0.703)	45.30** (0.852)	8.85** (0.167)
9	Hong Kong	25.80** (0.777)	37.30** (0.940)	9.14** (0.247)
10	Malaysia	17.31** (0.529)	30.33** (0.536)	11.09** (0.299)
11	Others	13.88** (0.268)	22.80** (0.293)	7.82** (0.263)
12	Total	13.69** (0.337)	21.73** (0.217)	7.07** (0.254)

* Significant at 5% level, ** Significant at 1% level

Figures in the parenthesis are standard errors

CAGR analyzed from 2009-10 to 2019-20 due to zero exports during 2008-09

CAGR analyzed from 2006-07 to 2019-20 due to zero exports during 2005-06

The analysis of export quantity growth rates for grapes revealed interesting findings across different destinations. Malaysia exhibited a positive and significant growth rate of 17.31 per cent per annum at the 1 per cent level, followed closely by Germany with a growth rate of 16.06 per cent, also significant at the 1 per cent level. In the case of Bangladesh, the growth rate in export quantity was 16.15 per cent, which was significant at the 5 per cent level. Furthermore, positive and significant growth rates were observed for grape exports to other destinations, with a growth rate of 13.88 per cent per annum. Overall, the study period showed a significant annual growth rate of

13.69 per cent in the quantity of grape exports from India, indicating a positive and notable trend in export performance at the 1 per cent level.

The analysis of growth rates in grape export values across different destinations revealed fascinating trends. Thailand exhibited the highest growth rate, with an impressive annual increase of 45.30 per cent in the value of grape exports. Russia closely followed with a substantial growth rate of 39.6 per cent per year. Both of these growth rates were statistically significant at the 1 per cent level, highlighting the considerable expansion in the value of grape exports to these countries. On the other hand, the UAE and the UK displayed the lowest growth rates in grape export values, recording rates of 12.15 per cent and 12.17 per cent per year, respectively. In contrast, Hong Kong and Malaysia experienced remarkable growth rates of 37.3 per cent and 30.33 per cent per year, respectively, indicating a strong market demand and a notable surge in the value of grape exports to these destinations.

During the study period, there was a noteworthy growth rate of 21.73 per cent per annum in the total value of grape exports, which was statistically significant at the 1 per cent level. Additionally, exports to other destinations showed a positive and significant growth rate of 22.8 per cent per annum in the value of grape exports. This indicates a robust expansion and increasing value of grape exports to diverse markets beyond the major destinations. The data underscores the overall positive performance of India's grape export sector, as it demonstrates consistent growth in the value of grape exports to both major and other destinations. The steady and significant growth rates signify the effectiveness of Indian exporters in tapping into various markets and meeting the demand for quality grapes worldwide.

During the study period, Malaysia demonstrated the highest growth rate of 11.09 per cent per annum in terms of the unit value of grapes exported from India. This growth rate was statistically significant at the 1 per cent level, indicating a notable increase in the value per quantity of grapes exported to Malaysia.

On the other hand, Russia, despite displaying remarkable growth rates in both the value and quantity of grape exports, showed a comparatively low growth rate of only 2.26 per cent per annum in terms of the unit value of exports. This growth rate was still statistically significant at the 1 per cent level, suggesting a steady but relatively slower increase in the value per quantity of grapes exported to Russia.

Netherlands, Saudi Arabia and the UAE, being consistent importers of Indian grapes, reported modest growth rates of 5.83 per cent, 5.89 per cent and 5.94

per cent per annum, respectively, in terms of the unit value of grape exports. These growth rates, along with their statistical significance, indicate a gradual rise in the value per quantity of grapes exported to these countries.

Noteworthy growth rates, accompanied by statistical significance, were observed for Hong Kong (9.14%), Thailand (8.85%), Bangladesh (8.65%) and Germany (8.48%) in terms of the unit value of grape exports. This implies a substantial increase in the value per quantity of grapes exported to these destinations.

These findings align closely with the results obtained by Kumar and Devaraj (2020), indicating a consistent pattern and supporting evidence of the trends in the unit value of grape exports to various destinations as reported in the study. The data reveals the dynamic and diverse market conditions for Indian grapes in different countries, with varying rates of increase in their value per quantity over the study period.

The unit value of exports to other importing countries, as well as the total grapes exports of India, demonstrated positive and significant growth rates of 7.82 per cent and 7.07 per cent per annum, respectively. These growth rates were statistically significant at the 1 per cent level, indicating a consistent increase in the value of grapes exported to these destinations over the study period.

Instability in Grapes Exports from India

The analysis of the variability in the trend of total grapes exports of India, conducted using the Cuddy-Della instability index, is presented in Table 3. It was found that the quantity of grapes exports exhibited an instability of 23.38 per cent over the study period, indicating fluctuations in the export volumes. Similarly, the unit value of grapes exports also showed a comparable instability of 24.82 per cent over the trend, suggesting fluctuations in the export prices. However, the value of grapes exports displayed slightly higher instability of 36.77 per cent during the study period, indicating greater volatility in the total export value.

Table 3: Cuddy- Della instability index (%) of grapes exports from India (2000-01 to 2019-20)

	Quantity	Value	Unit Value
CV (%)	62.28	95.68	48.42
Adjusted R Square	0.86	0.85	0.74
C-D II (%)	23.38	36.77	24.82

The analysis of year-to-year percentage instability in the quantity, value and unit value of grapes exports, conducted using the Coppock's instability index, is presented in Table 4. It was observed that among all the major destinations,

Bangladesh exhibited the highest instability in terms of quantity, value, and unit value of grapes imports from India. The quantity of grapes imports from India to Bangladesh displayed an annual instability of 231.41 per cent, indicating significant fluctuations in the import volumes. Similarly, the value of grapes imports from India to Bangladesh showed an annual instability of 231.75 per cent, indicating substantial fluctuations in the import values. Additionally, the unit value of grapes imports from India to Bangladesh exhibited an annual instability of 46.84 per cent, suggesting notable variations in the import prices.

In terms of grapes imports from India, Hong Kong demonstrated significant instability in both quantity and value. The quantity of grapes imports from India to Hong Kong exhibited a high annual instability rate of 172.27 per cent, indicating substantial fluctuations in import volumes. Similarly, the value of grapes imports from India to Hong Kong displayed a considerable annual instability rate of 209.19 per cent, indicating notable variations in import values. On the other hand, UAE emerged as the most stable destination among the others, with the lowest instability rates recorded in quantity, value, and unit value of grapes imports from India. Specifically, UAE displayed an annual instability rate of 19.99 per cent in quantity, indicating relatively stable import volumes. Additionally, the value of grapes imports from India to UAE showed an annual instability rate of 16.84 per cent, indicating a relatively stable import value. Moreover, the unit value of grapes imports from India to UAE exhibited the lowest annual instability rate of 13.54 per cent, suggesting a relatively stable import price. These results highlight the varying levels of instability observed in grapes imports from India across different destinations, with Hong Kong experiencing significant fluctuations and UAE demonstrating greater stability in the import market.

Despite experiencing significant instability in the quantity and value of grapes exports to the UK, the unit value of exports to the UK exhibited a remarkable level of stability compared to other major destinations. The unit value of exports to the UK demonstrated an annual instability percentage of only 9.61 per cent, indicating relatively consistent and steady export prices. In contrast, Russia and Thailand displayed relatively low instability in the unit value of grapes imports from India, despite having high instability in the value of imports. Specifically, Russia recorded a modest instability rate of 10.30 per cent per annum in the unit value of grapes imports, while Thailand exhibited a slightly higher but still relatively low instability rate of 12.18 per cent per annum

When considering other destinations collectively, they exhibited an instability of 44.17 per cent, 50.66 per cent, and 23.03 per cent per annum in the quantity, value and unit value of Indian grapes exports, respectively. The overall instability of grapes exports was moderately high, with the quantity and value of exports experiencing instability rates of 33.90 per cent and 31.36 per cent per annum, respectively. In contrast, the unit value of grapes exports displayed relatively low instability, recording an annual rate of 14.96 per cent. These findings indicate that while there is some variability in the exports of Indian grapes, the unit value remains relatively stable. Notably, the instability index results in this study were slightly lower than those reported by Indhushree *et al.* (2017), whose research covered a study period from 1988 to 2016. Their study found that grapes exports exhibited Coppock's instability index rates of 41.1 per cent, 44.4 per cent and 24.8 per cent per annum in value, quantity, and unit value of exports, respectively. This suggests that over the years, grapes exports have become more stable in terms of their variability and fluctuations.

Table 4: Country wise Coppock's instability index (%) of India's grapes exports (2000-01 to 2019-20)

Sr. No.	Country	Quantity	Value	Unit Value
1	Netherland	42.80	49.47	14.33
2	Russia #	73.11	72.83	10.30
3	UK	46.54	46.99	9.61
4	Bangladesh	231.41	231.75	46.84
5	Germany	96.50	83.51	23.49
6	UAE	19.99	16.84	13.54
7	Saudi Arabia	59.54	44.26	26.59
8	Thailand ##	52.59	64.70	12.18
9	Hong Kong	172.27	209.19	25.26
10	Malaysia	71.22	82.34	44.17
11	Others	44.17	50.66	23.03
12	Total	33.90	31.36	14.96

Instability analyzed from 2009-10 to 2019-20 due to zero exports during 2008-09
Instability analyzed from 2006-07 to 2019-20 due to zero exports during 2005-06

The analysis of the geographical concentration index was conducted for the selected commodities by examining the value of exports data for a specific commodity to various destinations within a particular year. The Hirschman concentration index was utilized for this purpose to determine the level of geographical concentration

The Hirschman geographical concentration index was computed for the selected commodities during their respective study periods to assess the level of diversification or concentration. A higher value of the Hirschman index indicates a lower degree of diversification (higher concentration) for the commodity, while a lower value indicates a higher level of diversification. The calculated Hirschman geographical concentration index for grapes were presented in Table 5.

The concentration index for grape exports from India varied between 52.31 per cent and 39.67 per cent. The lowest level of diversification was observed in the year 2000-01, with a concentration index of 52.31 per cent. Over the years, the concentration index gradually decreased, reaching 38.67 per cent in 2011-12. However, it then increased to 47.64 per cent in 2015-16 before gradually decreasing again. Overall, there was a decreasing trend in the concentration index during the study period, indicating that India's grape exports have become more diversified over the years. These findings align closely with the results reported by Indhushree *et al.* (2017).

The decreasing trend in the concentration index of grape exports can likely be attributed to several factors. Initially, the export of grapes was limited to neighbouring countries due to the absence of precooling facilities, and developed countries such as the EU, USA, and Germany had concerns regarding pesticide residue. However, over time, significant measures were taken to address these concerns by implementing improved agricultural practices and ensuring compliance with pesticide residue regulations (Idris *et al.*, 2015).

Table 5: Hirschman geographical concentration index (%) of selected commodities

Year	Grapes
2000-01	52.31
2001-02	50.71
2002-03	49.87
2003-04	43.34
2004-05	46.87
2005-06	45.02
2006-07	45.48
2007-08	50.57
2008-09	46.08
2009-10	46.41
2010-11	40.07
2011-12	38.67
2012-13	40.85
2013-14	43.36
2014-15	44.09
2015-16	47.64
2016-17	39.98
2017-18	40.95
2018-19	40.13
2019-20	41.12

The export performance ratio, also known as the revealed comparative advantage (RCA), was computed for the selected commodities. Due to the unavailability of world trade data on a financial year basis, calendar year data was utilized to determine the RCA. Additionally, the revealed symmetric advantage (RSCA) was calculated based on the RCA values obtained for each commodity. A positive RSCA value indicates the presence of a comparative advantage, while a negative value signifies the absence of a comparative advantage or a comparative disadvantage.

Revealed Comparative Advantage of Grapes Exports from India

Revealed comparative advantage (RCA) and revealed symmetric comparative advantage (RSCA) for the export of grapes from India during the period from 2001 to 2019 are illustrated in Table 6 and are visually represented in Figure 2.

From the year 2001 to 2013, the revealed comparative advantage (RCA) values for grapes exports from India were found to be below unity, indicating that India had a comparative disadvantage in this sector. This is further supported by the negative values of the revealed symmetric comparative advantage (RSCA) during those years. However, there was an increasing trend observed in RCA values during the period, with values of 0.37 in 2001 and 0.82 in 2013, suggesting that India was gradually gaining its comparative advantage in grapes exports. In 2014, the RSCA value turned positive (RCA>1), indicating that India had successfully achieved a comparative advantage in grapes exports that year. Subsequently, the RSCA value remained positive, except for 2015.

The analysis of the revealed symmetric comparative advantage (RSCA) values for grapes exports from India revealed an increasing trend in positive values. This indicates that India has been steadily gaining a stronger comparative advantage in grapes exports over the years. These findings align with the results reported by Chakraborty (2020), further confirming the growing competitive position of India in the grapes export market

Table 6: Revealed comparative advantage and revealed symmetric comparative advantage of India's grapes exports

Year	RCA	RSCA
2001	0.37	-0.46
2002	0.54	-0.30
2003	0.62	-0.24
2004	0.47	-0.36
2005	0.73	-0.15
2006	0.78	-0.12
2007	0.63	-0.23

Year	RCA	RSCA
2008	0.93	-0.04
2009	0.73	-0.16
2010	0.89	-0.06
2011	0.49	-0.34
2012	0.65	-0.22
2013	0.82	-0.10
2014	1.09	0.04
2015	0.74	-0.15
2016	1.43	0.18
2017	1.57	0.22
2018	1.57	0.22
2019	1.79	0.28

Study of Export Competitiveness

The nominal protection coefficient, considered the most effective measure for evaluating price competitiveness of exported commodities, was employed to assess the competitiveness of the selected commodities. Specifically, the nominal protection coefficient was calculated for a three-year period from 2017-18 to 2019-20. The results of the study of export competitiveness of the grapes export is given in the following sub-headings.

Competitiveness of Grapes Exports from India

The results of the nominal protection coefficient analysis for the exports of grapes from India are presented in Table 7. The NPC values calculated for all three years of the study were found to be less than one. Specifically, during the years 2017-18 and 2019-20, the NPC values were equal to 0.81, indicating a relatively low level of price competitiveness. In contrast, during the year 2018-19, the NPC value was slightly higher at 0.97, suggesting a slightly improved price competitiveness compared to the other two years.

Table 7: Nominal protection coefficient of grapes exports from India (2017-18 to 2019-20)

Year	Domestic Price (₹/q)	FOB Price (₹/q)	Average Marketing Expenses (₹/q)	International Reference Price/ Border price (₹/q)	NPC
2017-18	6321.11	10094.23	2312.67	7781.57	0.81
2018-19	6809.22	9487.73	2432.87	7054.86	0.97
2019-20	7014.65	11238.90	2555.61	8683.29	0.81

The observation of NPC values less than unity indicates that the domestic prices of grapes in India are relatively lower compared to the international reference prices. Specifically, during the years 2017-18 and 2019-20, India had an export advantage of 19 per cent (calculated as 1 - 0.81 x 100), suggesting a significant competitive edge in the export of grapes. However, during the year 2018-19, the export advantage was relatively lower at 3 per cent (1 - 0.97 x 100). These findings highlight that India is export competitive in the grapes market and there is potential to further enhance its grapes exports. These results align closely with the findings of Mokashi (2012) and Deshmukh (2015).

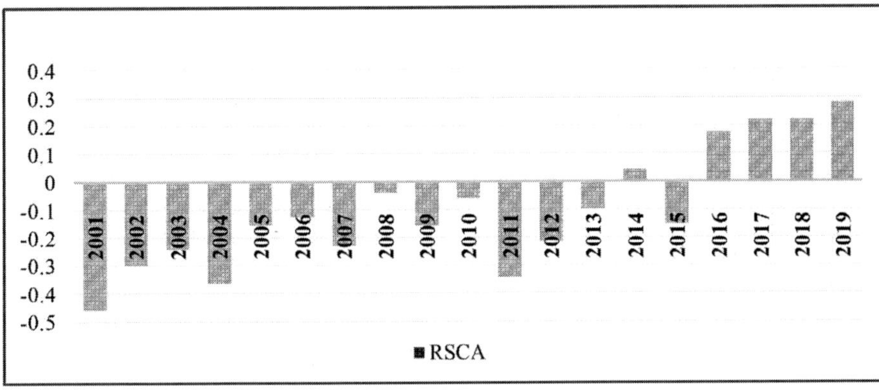

Fig. 2: Revealed symmetric comparative advantage of India's grapes exports

Study of Direction of Trade

The analysis of structural change in the trade pattern was conducted using Markov chain analysis, which is a method suitable for studying systems with a single outcome variable. Transitional probabilities were calculated based on the export quantity data over the past ten years. The top seven importing countries were selected based on their export quantity during the year 2019-20, while the export quantities of other countries were grouped together under the category of 'others'. The Transition Probability Matrix (TPM) was estimated using a linear programming framework, specifically the method of minimizing the Mean Absolute Deviation. A linear programming problem was formulated using Visual Basic in MS Excel and the software version 5.5.2.5 of LDSolve IDE was utilized to solve the linear programming problem. Obtained TPMs were used to obtain the predicted share of export and it was compared with actual shares using modified chi-square test. These results of the Markov chain analysis are presented in the following sub headings.

Table 8: Direction of Trade of Grapes Exports from India

	Netherland	Bangladesh	Russia	U K	UAE	Germany	Saudi Arabia	Others
Netherland	**0.5311**	0.0000	0.1104	0.0000	0.0000	0.0301	0.0670	0.2615
Bangladesh	0.1867	**0.3680**	0.1067	0.0530	0.1563	0.0000	0.0453	0.0840
Russia	0.5435	0.0000	**0.2534**	0.2031	0.0000	0.0000	0.0000	0.0000
U K	0.0000	0.5345	0.0000	**0.0000**	0.4249	0.0405	0.0000	0.0000
UAE	0.2917	0.0000	0.0000	0.6188	**0.0895**	0.0000	0.0000	0.0000
Germany	0.0000	0.0000	0.0000	0.0000	0.0000	**0.5784**	0.0000	0.4216
Saudi Arabia	0.4629	0.0000	0.3317	0.2054	0.0000	0.0000	**0.0000**	0.0000
Others	0.0000	0.3610	0.1552	0.0000	0.0000	0.0000	0.0854	**0.3984**

In terms of grape exports from India, Bangladesh exhibited a retention rate of 36.80% while losing 18.67 per cent and 15.63 per cent of its market share to Netherland and UAE, respectively. However, Bangladesh gained a substantial 54.35 per cent share from Russia and a 46.29 per cent share from Saudi Arabia.

Russia, on the other hand, demonstrated a retention rate of 25.34 per cent, but lost the majority of its market share (54.35%) to Netherland, and the remaining 20.31 per cent to the UK.

Despite the UK not retaining any of its market share and losing 53.45 per cent and 42.49 per cent to Russia and UAE, respectively, it gained 61.88 per cent of the UAE's market share and 20.54 per cent of Saudi Arabia's market share during the study period.

The United Arab Emirates (UAE) exhibited a relatively low retention rate of 8.95 per cent after losing a significant portion of its market share to the UK and the remaining 29.17 per cent to Netherland. Saudi Arabia experienced a complete loss of market share, with 46.29 per cent going to Netherland, 33.17 per cent to Russia and 20.54 per cent to the UK, resulting in zero retention.

The remaining importing countries displayed a retention rate of 39.84 per cent and gained a 42.16 per cent share from Germany 26.15 per cent share from Netherland and 8.40 per cent share from Bangladesh.

Export Market Projections of Grapes

The expected shares of grapes exports from India were determined by utilizing the transitional probability matrix. Subsequently, these expected shares were compared to the actual shares of exports and the results are displayed in Table 9. Upon examination, it is evident that the disparities between the actual and predicted shares of grape exports were generally minimal.

Table 9: Actual and predicted shares (%) of grapes exports from India to major destinations

Countries	Netherland		Bangladesh		Russia		U K		UAE		Germany		Saudi Arabia		Others	
Years	A	P	A	P	A	P	A	P	A	P	A	P	A	P	A	P
2010-11	19.67	-	41.17	-	2.20	-	7.48	-	9.71	-	0.70	-	3.50	-	15.56	-
2011-12	19.38	23.79	37.57	24.77	4.86	10.70	6.92	9.36	10.69	10.48	0.63	1.30	4.51	4.51	15.44	15.10
2012-13	25.48	25.15	23.10	23.10	11.27	11.27	10.52	10.52	9.77	9.77	1.04	1.23	4.19	4.32	14.64	14.64
2013-14	28.76	28.76	19.41	19.41	14.52	11.79	10.42	10.42	6.52	8.96	1.51	1.79	4.52	4.00	14.34	14.87
2014-15	34.78	30.78	3.68	17.89	13.08	12.65	13.98	8.94	12.23	8.05	2.71	2.16	4.03	4.03	15.50	15.50
2015-16	37.99	31.70	5.90	14.42	9.38	11.29	13.27	11.25	8.81	7.61	3.18	3.18	4.14	3.82	17.32	16.72
2016-17	27.72	30.86	19.20	15.52	11.26	11.26	6.84	8.52	7.35	7.35	5.27	3.52	3.68	4.29	18.67	18.67
2017-18	31.06	28.27	2.70	17.46	14.58	12.08	9.88	8.61	7.21	6.57	8.74	4.16	5.04	4.32	20.80	18.52
2018-19	29.36	29.36	18.86	13.78	12.31	12.31	7.15	8.60	5.19	5.27	6.39	6.39	3.74	3.98	17.00	20.32
2019-20	29.05	29.05	16.90	16.90	12.25	12.25	7.48	7.48	6.26	6.45	4.50	4.87	4.50	4.27	19.05	18.73

Goodness of fit: χCal^2=4.91; χ_tab^2 at 56 degrees of freedom at 5% = 74.47, A-Actual and P-Predicted

Table 10: Actual and predicted quantities ('000 metric tons) of grapes exports from India to major destinations

Countries Years	Netherland		Bangladesh		Russia		U K		UAE		Germany		Saudi Arabia		Others	
	A	P	A	P	A	P	A	P	A	P	A	P	A	P	A	P
2010-11	18.19	-	38.05	-	2.04	-	6.91	-	8.97	-	0.65	-	3.24	-	14.39	-
2011-12	18.38	21.99	35.64	22.89	4.61	9.89	6.56	8.65	10.14	9.69	0.60	1.20	4.28	4.17	14.64	13.96
2012-13	35.91	23.86	32.56	21.91	15.89	10.69	14.83	9.98	13.77	9.27	1.46	1.17	5.91	4.10	20.64	13.89
2013-14	46.08	40.54	31.11	27.36	23.28	15.62	16.70	14.69	10.45	12.62	2.42	2.53	7.24	5.64	22.98	20.96
2014-15	32.82	49.33	3.47	28.67	12.34	20.27	13.19	14.33	11.55	12.89	2.56	3.46	3.81	6.46	14.63	24.84
2015-16	50.39	29.92	7.83	13.61	12.45	10.65	17.60	10.62	11.69	7.18	4.22	3.00	5.49	3.61	22.98	15.78
2016-17	55.01	40.94	38.11	20.58	22.34	14.94	13.58	11.31	14.60	9.75	10.47	4.67	7.31	5.69	37.06	24.77
2017-18	58.46	56.11	5.07	34.66	27.43	23.97	18.59	17.09	13.57	13.03	16.45	8.26	9.48	8.58	39.15	36.76
2018-19	72.26	55.25	46.42	25.94	30.29	23.17	17.60	16.19	12.77	9.91	15.74	12.03	9.20	7.49	41.85	38.25
2019-20	56.27	71.50	32.74	41.60	23.74	30.15	14.48	18.41	12.13	15.88	8.72	11.99	8.71	10.52	36.90	46.10
2020-21	-	56.47	-	33.12	-	24.33	-	15.85	-	12.36	-	7.32	-	8.40	-	35.84
2021-22	-	56.89	-	33.60	-	24.28	-	16.07	-	13.02	-	6.58	-	8.34	-	34.91
2022-23	-	57.34	-	33.56	-	24.20	-	16.48	-	13.25	-	6.17	-	8.31	-	34.38

A-Actual and P-Predicted

The computed chi-square value (4.91) was found to be lower than the critical table value (74.47) at 56 degrees of freedom and 5 per cent level of significance. This indicates that the observed and predicted shares of grape exports from India exhibit identical distribution. Consequently, it can be inferred that the actual shares align consistently with the predicted shares of exports to major destinations. This validation confirms the effectiveness of the Markov chain model in estimating future exports to prominent countries using transitional probabilities.

Projected quantities of grape exports to major destinations were derived by performing matrix multiplication between the transitional probability matrix and the original exports series of the significant importing countries for subsequent years. The forecasting was extended until the year 2022-23 and the outcomes are displayed in Table 10.

Based on the projections, Netherland is anticipated to remain the primary importer of Indian grapes, with the largest share. It is estimated to import 56.47 thousand metric tons of grapes from India in 2020-21, which is expected to increase to 56.89 thousand metric tons in 2021-22 and further to 57.34 thousand metric tons in 2022-23.

The export share to Bangladesh is also predicted to grow, reaching 33.12 thousand metric tons in 2020-21 and further increasing to 33.60 thousand metric tons in 2021-22. Conversely, Russia's imports are projected to slightly decrease over the next three years, declining from 24.33 thousand metric tons in 2020-21 to 24.20 thousand metric tons in 2022-23

The exports to the UK are projected to increase from 15.85 thousand metric tons in 2020-21 to 16.48 thousand metric tons in 2022-23. Similarly, the exports to the UAE are also expected to rise from 12.36 thousand metric tons to 13.25 thousand metric tons over the next three years. However, there is an anticipated decrease in exports to Germany, Saudi Arabia, and other export destinations during the predicted years.

Conclusion

CAGR of total quantity and value of fresh grapes exports during the study period was 13.69 per cent and 21.73 per cent, respectively. Destination wise analysis of CAGR showed that, all the major destinations recorded positive and significant growth rate in terms of quantity, value and unit value of exports. The average instability over the trend in total fresh grapes exports during the study period was 23.38 per cent, 36.77 per cent and 24.82 per cent in quantity, value and unit value of exports respectively. Average year to year instability in total fresh grapes exports was 33.90 per cent, 31.36 per cent and 14.96 per cent, respectively in quantity, value and unit value of exports. Among the major destinations, highest instability was recorded by Bangladesh and Hong Kong. UAE was found to be most stable destination for Indian fresh grapes exports.

The decreasing trend seen in case of geographical concentration index of fresh grapes exports from India during the study period, which shows that the India's grapes exports is becoming more and more diversified over the years. India's grapes exports was found to have comparative disadvantage during year 2001 to 2015 except during 2014, and there was decreasing trend in disadvantage. From the year 2016 to 2019, India had comparative advantage and increasing trend was seen in its RSCA values. Exports of fresh grapes from India was price competitive during the year 2017-18 to 2019-20. The values of NPC obtained were 0.81, 0.97 and 0.81 during the year 2017-18, 2018-19 and 2019-20 respectively Study of direction of trade of fresh grapes exports from India (2010-11 to 2019-20) showed that Germany and Netherland were the most loyal Importers. Whereas UK and Saudi Arabia showed no retention of their shares during the study period. Export projections of fresh grapes shows that Netherland will continue to be the largest exporter of fresh grapes from India during next three years (2020-21 to 2022-23). There will be increasing in exports to UK and UAE. Decreasing trend will be seen in exports to Russia, Germany and Saudi Arabia. Mixed trend will be observed in exports to Netherland, Bangladesh and remaining importers together.

References

Agricultural and Processed food Products Export Development Authority (APEDA). (2020). AgriXchange Portal. Ministry of Commerce & Industry. Government of India. Retrieved from https://doi.org/10.5958/0974-0279.2016.00009.4

Deshmukh, B. J. (2015). Economic Analysis of Production, Marketing and Export of Grapes from Maharashtra (Doctoral thesis, Mahatma Phule Krishi Vidyapeeth, Rahuri, Maharashtra). Retrieved from https://krishikosh.egranth.ac.in/displaybitstream?handle=1/5810161934&fileid=2bee66e2-d2e1-4713-b099-10e27e9bf379

Directorate of Economics & Statistics. (2020). Pocket Book of Agricultural Statistics 2019. Department of Agriculture, Cooperation & Farmers Welfare. Government of India. Retrieved from https://eands.dacnet.nic.in/PDF/Pocket%20Book%202019.pdf

Idris, S., Singh, A., & Praveen, K. V. (2015). Trade Competitiveness and Impact of Food Safety Regulations on Market Access of India's Horticultural Trade. Agricultural Economics Research Review, 28(2), 301–309.

Indhushree, A., Kuruvila, A., Thomas, J., & Bastine, L. C. (2017). Fruit and vegetable exports in the post-liberalization era: The Indian experience. Journal of Horticultural Science, 12 (2), 133–142. Retrieved from https://jhs.iihr.res.in/index.php/jhs/article/download/14/6

International Trade Centre. (2019). Trade Map. [Data File]. Retrieved from https://www.trademap.org

Kumar, A. D. S., & Devaraj, M. (2020). Export performance of grapes in India. Journal of Research ANGRAU, 48 (1), 37-45.

Ministry of Finance. (2021). Economic Survey 2020-21, Statistical Appendix. Government of India. Retrieved from https://www.indiabudget.gov.in/economicsurvey/doc/Statistical-Appendix-in-English.pdf

Mokashi, P. K. (2012). An Economic Analysis of Export Potential of Grapes from Northern Karnataka (Master's thesis University of Agricultural Sciences, Dharwad, Karnataka). Retrieved from https://krishikosh.egranth.ac.in/displaybitstream?handle=1/86286&fileid=0e7617e5-8ebf-455e-af89-6b676e4bd9ed

World Bank. (2020). World Integrated Trade Solutions. India Trade Statistics. Retrieved from https://wits.worldbank.org/CountryProfile/en/IND

Website referred

www.faostat.org

4

Status and Trade Dynamics of Castor from India

Ganga Devi*, Mohit Kumar[1] Pooja Nautiyal[2], Hardi Patel[3] and Alpa Karmur[4]

**Department of Agricultural Economics, B.A. College of Agriculture Anand Agricultural University, Anand, Gujarat*
[1]Department of Agricultural Economics, B.A. College of Agriculture Anand Agricultural University, Anand, Gujarat
[2, 3 & 4] Department of Agricultural Economics, B.A. College of Agriculture Anand Agricultural University, Anand, Gujarat

Abstract

India holds a dominant position in the global production and export of castor, accounting for nearly 88% of global and leading the international the international castor oil trade. This chapter investigates the status of castor production and trade dynamics, highlighting India's evolving role in commercial agriculture and export-oriented strategies. Castor, a non-edible oilseed with significant industrial applications, is primarily cultivated in Gujarat, Rajasthan, and Andhra Pradesh. The study explores trends in area, production and yield across states and districts, alongside export trends over a 15 year period (2006-06 to 2019-20). Results show positive growth in export quantity, value and unit price, despite fluctuations, supported by favourable policies and quality improvements. Using the Markov chain model, the direction of trade analysis reveals China as the most stable and dominant importer, followed by Netherlands and France. The USA also shows emerging potential. Instability indices indicate relatively low volatility in trade metrics. The finding suggest that while India maintains a strong global presence, strategic efforts are needed to sustain existing markets and explore new opportunities, especially in emerging economies offering better prices and reliability.

Keywords: *Castor Oil Exports, High-Value Commercial Crops, Direction of Trade, Global and Castor Trade Dynamics*

Background

Over the years, Indian agriculture has experienced remarkable transformations, reflecting significant trends of extensive commercialization and diversification within the sector. Indian agriculture changed a lot and became more commercial. It showed strength as a bright sector, growing by 3.4 per cent and contributed nearly 20 per cent to the country's economy, even when the whole economy shrank by 7.2 per cent in the pandemic year (2020-21). National efforts in the agriculture sector have sparked enthusiasm among various groups, including research scientists, policymakers, corporate players and especially farmers. The aim is to bring new energy and speed up agricultural growth. The primary strategies involve transforming agriculture into a more commercial enterprise, encouraging farmers to become entrepreneurs, promoting export-oriented farming and prioritizing ways to increase farmers' income. In recent times, Indian agriculture has been experiencing a significant change in its perspective and priorities. There has been a shift from focusing solely on food security to now emphasizing income security. Additionally, there's a transition from traditional crops to commercial crops and a move away from relying on mono-cropping to promoting crop diversification. With these developments in mind, an effort has been made to assess the present situation of castor production and export in major producing countries globally.

Production and Export Scenario of High-Valued Commercial Crops

India holds a dominant position as the primary producer of various high-value commercial crops at the global level. Presently, India occupies a pre-eminent status in the worldwide production and export of high-value commercial crops, including chilli, turmeric and castor. However, in the case of tobacco, India is ranked second both in production and exports.

Table 1: Status of Indian high-value commercial crops at the global level

Crops	Production			Export			
	Production	India's Share (%)	India's Rank	Volume of Exports (lakh tons)	India's Share	Value of exports (Rs. Crore)	India's Rank
Chilli	20.49	42	First	5.57	56	8582	First
Turmeric	13.31	85	First	1.53	76	1784	First
Castor	16.47	88	First	6.90	87	7805	First
Tobacco	7.58	13	Second	2.12	9	6306	Second

Source: Faostat, 2022

Among the major producing countries worldwide, India holds a dominant position, contributing significantly to global production. Specifically, India accounts for a substantial share of 88 per cent of the world's production. At present, India is the leading exporter in the global market for various high-value commercial crops. Notably, it holds the top position in the export of chilli (56%), turmeric (76%) and castor (87%). Moreover, India ranks second in the global export of tobacco, with a share of 9 per cent. This highlights India's strong presence and leadership in the international trade of these high-value commercial crops (Table 1). Therefore, this chapter looks into the production along with the export status and destinations of castor crop.

Castor

The Castor plant (Ricinus communis L.) originated in Africa. During the 19th century, its cultivation began on a large scale in countries like India, USA, UK and Russia primarily as an industrial oilseed crop. The demand for castor oil also witnessed a steady rise of approximately 3-5 per cent per year (source: www.castoroil.in). This increased demand and importance of castor oil led to a surge in dedicated exploratory research on castor worldwide.

Economic Importance

Castor is recognized as a crucial industrial non-edible oilseed crop. It has a substantial oil content, with an average of 50-60 per cent of oil that can be extracted from the commercial castor crop (source: www.castoroil.in/extraction/extraction.html). Indian castor, in particular, contains approximately 27.6 per cent protein, 11.8 per cent ash and 11.3 per cent fibre content. These properties make castor an important resource for various industrial applications given its high oil yield and significant protein and fibre content.

Castor Production Scenario

Castor is cultivated on a commercial scale in more than 30 countries worldwide. However, the area under castor cultivation has been subject to regular fluctuations in recent years. For instance, the area of land dedicated to castor cultivation was 14,30,515 hectares in 2016, 13,35,838 hectares in 2017 and 12,96,855 hectares in 2018 (source: www.faostat.com).

Table 2: Top five castor producing countries

	Production (tonnes)					
Year	**India**	**Mozambique**	**Brazil**	**China**	**Myanmar**	**World**
2014-15	1811000	73374.50	42158.50	40000.00	11794.50	2038595
	(88.83)	(3.59)	(2.06)	(1.96)	(0.57)	(100)
2015-16	1564000	78399.50	35677.50	38500.00	12213.00	1988304
	(78.66)	(3.94)	(1.79)	(1.93)	(0.61)	(100)
2016-17	1472000	81180.50	34500.00	19050.50	12051.50	1585794
	(92.82)	(5.12)	(2.18)	(1.20)	(0.76)	(100)
2017-18	1383000	84017.50	13852.50	29500.00	12053.00	1670903
	(82.77)	(5.03)	(0.83)	(1.77)	(0.72)	(100)
2018-19	1198000	85436.00	14224.00	27000.00	12068.00	1765067
	(67.87)	(4.84)	(0.81)	(1.53)	(0.69)	(100)
2018-19	1196680 (84.61)	72378.75 (5.11)	27412 (1.93)	36000 (2.5)	11798.25 (0.83)	1414190 (100)
2019-20	1842020 (89.78)	72848.92 (3.55)	35800 (1.74)	17000 (0.82)	11730.07 (0.57)	2051523 (100)
2021-22	1647000 (88.46)	72783.38 (3.90)	35195 (1.89)	21000 (1.12)	11696.5 (0.62)	1861700 (100)

Source: http://www.fao.org/faostat/en/#data/QC/visualize

Note: Figures in parenthesis indicate percentages to total world castor production

According to Food and Agriculture Organisation (FAO) during 2021-22 (Table 2), India ranked first with 1647000 tonnes of castor production followed by Mozambique, Brazil, China mainland and Myanmar. Beside these, other countries like Thailand, Madagascar, Ethiopia, Paraguay, Indonesia, Tanzania *etc.,* also hold important position in term of world castor production.

Castor Production Scenario in India

India has continuously expanded castor cultivation from 4.86 lakh ha in 1961 to 9.38 lakh ha in 2019, which indicate 52 per cent expansion in castor area, especially in Gujarat and to some extent in Andhra Pradesh and Rajasthan. Gujarat, Rajasthan and Andhra Pradesh are the major castor growing states contributing around 91 and 97 per cent to the countries area and production, respectively (Rai *et al.,* 2016). Gujarat ranks first in castor production. About 73 per cent castor oil in India came from Gujarat state only (Gondalia *et al.,* 2020).

Table 3: State wise area, production and yield of castor

Year	Area (000' hectares)					
	Gujarat	Rajasthan	Andhra Pradesh	Maharashtra	Orissa	Telangana
2014-15	715.00	226.30	48.00	17.00	10.90	51.00
2015-16	714.00	191.40	51.00	21.00	10.50	48.00
2016-17	541.00	142.47	33.00	7.00	8.91	46.00
2017-18	585.60	142.46	32.00	6.00	7.77	28.00
2018-19	521.88	140.57	37.00	12.50	7.24	20.00
2019-20	736.6	204.3	38.0	10.6	6.8	28.0
2020-21	652.92	177.98	16.00	10.30	6.52	11.00
Production (000' tonnes)						
2014-15	1456.00	335.10	27.00	4.00	7.00	30.00
2015-16	1413.00	269.90	29.00	5.00	6.60	17.00
2016-17	1221.00	190.68	16.00	2.10	5.62	26.00
2017-18	1333.33	167.82	20.96	1.42	4.91	26.24
2018-19	944.08	207.62	15.36	3.64	4.59	15.24
2019-20	1431.93	326.50	25.99	3.24	4.24	36.68
2020-21	1345.02	276.22	6.46	4.33	4.13	3.72
Yield (kg per hectare)						
2014-15	2036	1481	563	235	638	588
2015-16	1979	1410	568	238	632	354
2016-17	2072	1338	485	304	631	578
2017-18	2279	1178	655	236	632	937
2018-19	1809	1477	415	291	634	762
2019-20	1944	1598	684	305	625	1310
2020-21	2060	1552	404	420	633	338

Source: https://eands.dacnet.nic.in/APY_96_To_06.htm

Castor Production Scenario in Gujarat

In Gujarat Mahesana, Banaskantha, Patan, Ahmadabad *etc.*, are some of the major castor producing districts. During 2018-19, the total area under cultivation was highest in Mahesana district *i.e.*, 87184 hectares with total production of 192937 tonnes followed by Banaskantha with 60028 hectares area and 172216 tonnes production. Patan district covered an area of 58976 hectare with 113073 tonnes production (Table 4).

Table 4: Top five castor producing districts of Gujarat

Districts	Area (hectare)	Production (tonnes)
Mahesana	87184	192937
Banaskantha	60028	172216
Patan	58976	113073
Ahmadabad	54716	101379
Vadodara	48719	99225

Source: https://aps.dac.gov.in/APY/Public_Report1.aspx

Growth and Instability in Export of Castor

India produces almost 68 per cent of the global castor seed yield, holding the top position in both castor cultivation area and production worldwide. Additionally, India leads as the largest producer of castor oil. However, India does not export castor in its seed form; instead, the primary export is in the form of castor oil.

Table 5 presents the export trends of castor in India over a fifteen-year period, spanning from 2005-06 to 2019-20. The export quantity showed continuous fluctuations throughout the years. Starting from Rs. 2,33,324.09 thousand tonnes in 2005-06, it steadily rose to Rs. 6,51,409.56 thousand tonnes in 2017-18 but subsequently declined to Rs. 5,49,489.54 thousand tonnes in 2019-20. In contrast, the export value demonstrated a consistent increase from Rs. 84,502.87 lakhs in 2005-06 to Rs. 6,23,527.91 lakhs in 2017-18, after which it decreased to Rs. 5,78,248.64 lakhs in 2019-20. Moreover, the unit value of the commodity exhibited a continuous upward trend, rising from Rs. 36,217 per tonne in 2005-06 to Rs. 1,05,234 tonne in 2019-20.

Moreover, the variability in the given variables over the study period was calculated using the Cuddy – Della Valle index (Cuddy and Valle, 1978). The data presented in Table 5 indicates a positive and significant growth rate of 6.00 per cent in the export quantity of castor oil during the analyzed period. Similarly, the export value and unit value also experienced positive and significant growth rates of 15.00 and 8.00 per cent, respectively. Notably, the maximum growth rate was observed for the export value, whereas the minimum growth rate was observed for the export quantity. These findings align with the results obtained by Shanker (2013). The continuous growth in castor oil exports can potentially be attributed to important government initiatives aimed at enhancing castor exports, such as the introduction of Duty Entitlement Pass Book (DEPB) rates for castor and investments in research and development to produce superior quality castor seeds.

Table 5: Compound annual growth rate and instability index of export quantity, value and price of castor oil

Year	Export quantity (thousand tonnes)	Export value (Rs)	Unit value (Rs/tonne)
2005-06	2,33,324.09	84,502.87	36217
2006-07	2,71,595.83	98,690.24	36337
2007-08	2,57,515.13	1,15,116.56	44703
2008-09	3,31,665.43	1,94,165.03	58542
2009-10	3,68,433.06	1,98,732.04	53940
2010-11	3,94,771.85	2,72,910.80	69131
2011-12	4,55,282.46	4,15,615.41	91287
2012-13	5,27,465.25	3,96,654.17	75200
2013-14	5,05,339.63	3,99,546.69	79065
2014-15	5,05,819.68	4,30,408.04	85091
2015-16	5,43,485.77	4,21,394.05	77535
2016-17	5,54,931.91	4,13,589.56	74530
2017-18	6,51,409.56	6,23,527.91	95720
2018-19	5,74,132.96	5,65,782.63	98546
2019-20	5,49,489.54	5,78,248.64	105234
R^2	0.88	0.92	0.84
't' value	10.23	12.24	8.22
Mean	4,48,310.81	3,47,258.98	72072
Standard Deviation	130197.89	177247.26	22079.70
Coefficient of Variation	29.04	51.04	30.64
Compound Annual Growth Rate (%)	6.00**	15.00**	8.00**
Cuddy Della Valle Index (%)	10.02	14.96	12.78

** represent significant at 1 per cent probability level

The Cuddy-Della Valle Index was utilized to calculate the variability in export quantity, export value and unit value of castor oil over the fifteen-year period from 2005-06 to 2019-20. The instability index magnitudes were determined to be 10.02 per cent for export quantity, 14.96 per cent for export value and 12.78 per cent for the unit price of castor oil. Notably, all three variables, including export quantity, value, and unit value, exhibited low variability.

Among these three variables, the maximum variability was observed in the export value, followed by the unit price and export quantity. Growth trend of export quantity and value are mentioned in Figure 1 and Figure 2, respectively.

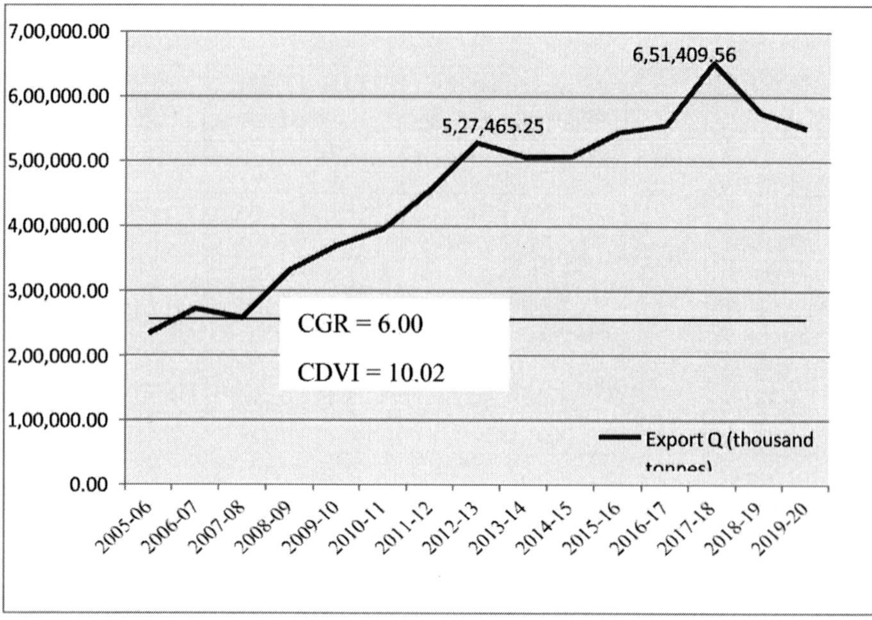

Fig. 1: Growth trend of export quantity of castor oil from India

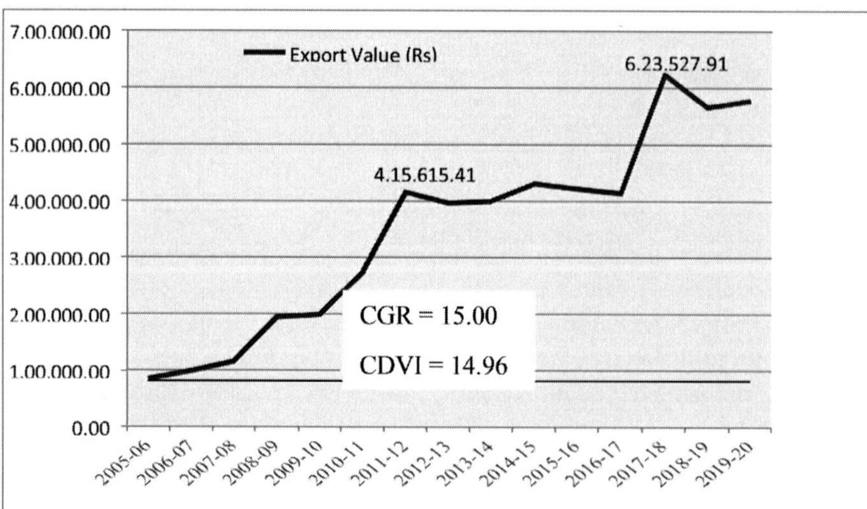

Fig. 2: Growth trend of export value of castor oil from India

Direction of Trade of Castor Oil

India occupies a prominent position in the global export of castor oil, with its primary export destinations being China, Netherlands, USA, Japan, France, Thailand, and UK, while the remaining countries are categorized under the 'others' group as shown in Table. 6. These major countries have been ranked based on both export quantity and export value.

China stands out as the largest importer of castor oil, accounting for approximately 42.59 per cent of the total quantity exported. Following China, the Netherlands receives 15.89 per cent, the USA 10.42 per cent, France 10.23 per cent, Japan 2.80 per cent, Thailand 2.75 per cent and the UK 1.68 per cent of the castor oil exports from India.

Table 6: Major importers of Indian castor oil during 2019-20

Country	Rank	Export quantity		Export Value	
		Thousand tonnes	Percent	Rs Lakh	Per cent
China	1	2,34,014.42	42.59	2,39,846.16	41.48
Netherlands	2	87,314.51	15.89	91,070.55	15.75
USA	3	57,244.76	10.42	62,420.99	10.79
France	4	56,189.89	10.23	58,870.46	10.18
Japan	5	15,407.63	2.80	16,461.19	2.85
Thailand	6	15,094.46	2.75	16,160.57	2.79
UK	7	9,252.38	1.68	10,173.92	1.76
Others (102)		74971.54	13.64	83244.76	14.40
Total		5,49,489.59	100	5,78,248.60	100

Source: Faostat, 2020

In the year 2019-20, India's castor oil exports resulted in a significant revenue of 5,78,248.60 lakh. Among the major export destinations, China emerged as the top importer, contributing 41.48 per cent to the total export value of castor oil. The Netherlands followed closely, accounting for 15.75 per cent, while the USA contributed 10.79 per cent and France 10.18 per cent. Japan, Thailand, UK, and other countries also played notable roles, with percentages of 2.85, 2.79, 1.76 and 14.40, respectively, in the total export value of Indian castor oil. These figures are depicted in Figure 3 and Figure 4, which illustrate the major export destinations of Indian castor oil based on quantity and value during the mentioned period.

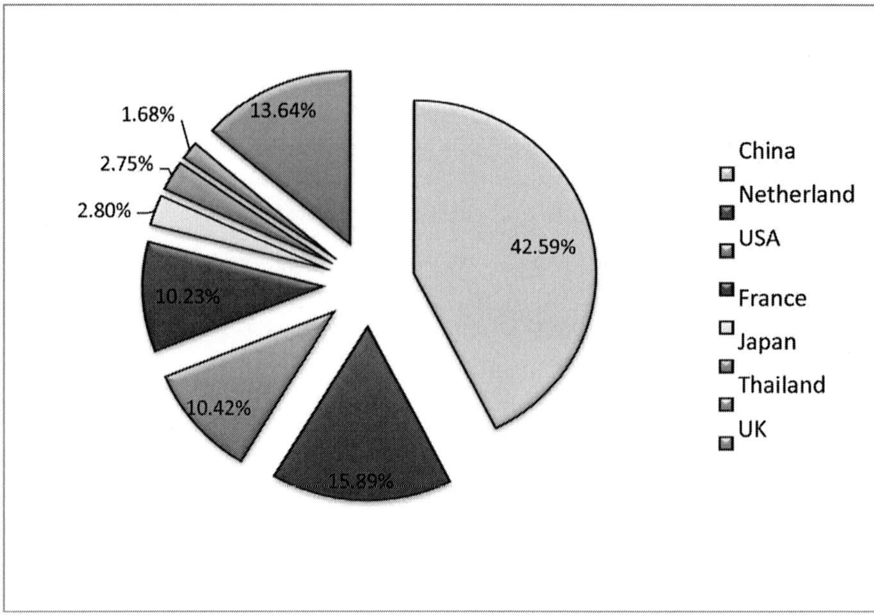

Fig. 3: Major export destinations of Indian castor oil (Quantity)

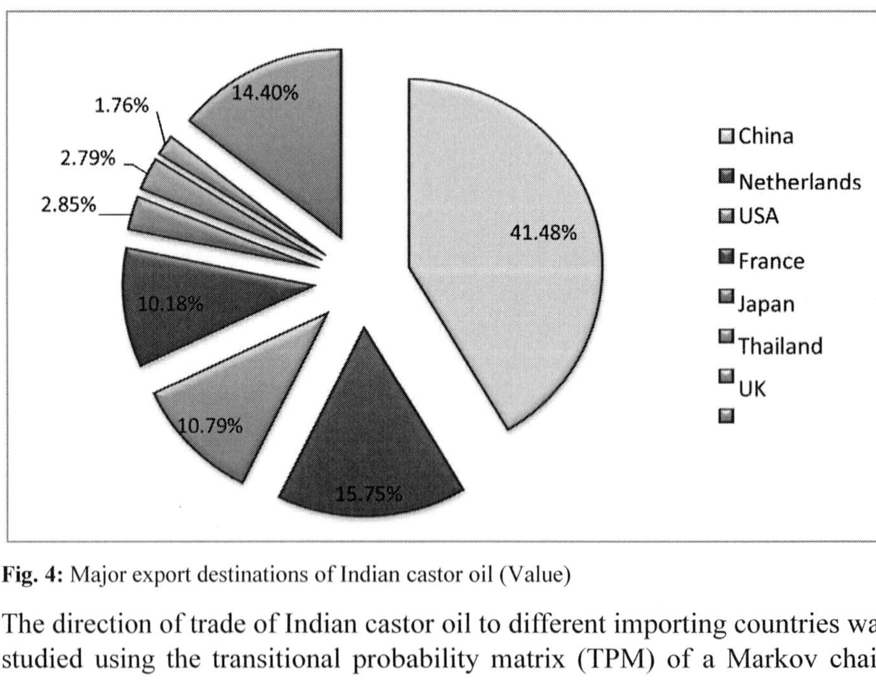

Fig. 4: Major export destinations of Indian castor oil (Value)

The direction of trade of Indian castor oil to different importing countries was studied using the transitional probability matrix (TPM) of a Markov chain model. The analysis was conducted using LINGO software. In Table 7, the transitional probabilities are provided, offering a clear understanding of the direction of trade during the fifteen-year period from 2005-06 to 2019-20.

The diagonal values of the TPM represent the probability of major importing countries retaining their share of imports over time. This indicates the likelihood of these countries continuing to be significant importers of Indian castor oil.

Furthermore, the row values of the TPM indicate the probability of major importing countries losing their market shares to other competing countries. This reveals the likelihood of these countries facing competition and potentially losing some portion of their imports to other destinations.

On the other hand, the column values of the TPM indicate the probability of major importing countries gaining import shares from other competing countries. This signifies the possibility of these countries expanding their market share by capturing imports that were previously directed to other destinations.

By analyzing these transitional probabilities, the direction of trade and the dynamics of import shares for Indian castor oil can be better understood over the specified fifteen-year period.

During the entire study period, China stood out as the largest importer of Indian castor, holding an impressive share of approximately 74.6 per cent of India's castor oil exports. Over the years, China gained significant market shares from various countries, including 54.1 per cent from Thailand, 32.4 per cent from the USA and 28.3 per cent from France. This highlights China's dominant position in the import market for Indian castor oil.

However, it's worth noting that China also experienced some losses in its market shares to other destinations. Specifically, it lost 7.5 per cent, 7.4 per cent, 5.5 per cent, 3.3 per cent and 1.6 per cent of its shares to "others," the Netherlands, Thailand, the USA, and the UK, respectively.

Interestingly, no other major importing country consistently retained its share of imports during the study period, further emphasizing China's strong position and dynamic nature of the castor oil trade market. These figures are detailed in Table 7 and visually represented in Figure 5.

Table 7: Direction of castor oil export in quantity from India (2005 to 2019)

Country	China	Netherl-ands	USA	France	Japan	Thailand	UK	Others
China	**0.746**	0.074	0.033	0.000	0.000	0.055	0.016	0.075
Netherlands	0.000	**0.060**	0.218	0.659	0.062	0.000	0.000	0.000
USA	0.324	0.493	**0.051**	0.000	0.081	0.000	0.050	0.000
France	0.283	0.375	0.072	**0.133**	0.019	0.108	0.002	0.008
Japan	0.000	0.000	0.008	0.390	**0.368**	0.000	0.079	0.155
Thailand	0.541	0.000	0.459	0.000	0.000	**0.000**	0.000	0.000
UK	0.000	0.824	0.176	0.000	0.000	0.000	**0.000**	0.000
Others	0.000	0.069	0.210	0.019	0.000	0.030	0.012	**0.661**

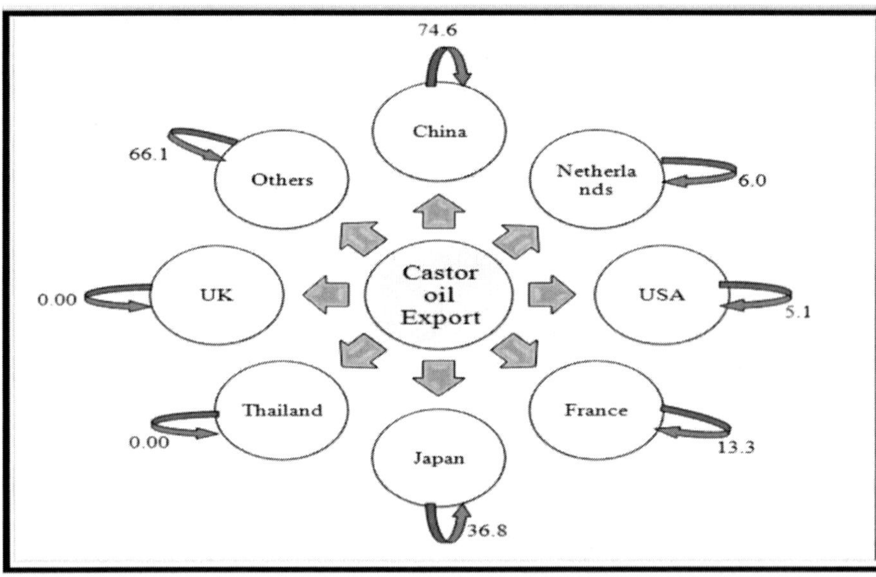

Fig. 5: Import shares of castor oil retained by major competing countries (quantity)

During the study period, a group of other countries, including Germany, Brazil, Belgium, Korea, Italy, Turkey, Russia, UAE, Egypt, Canada, Australia and more, collectively retained a significant import share of 66.1 per cent of Indian castor oil. These countries experienced changes in their market shares due to various factors.

From China, they gained a 7.5 per cent share of Indian castor oil exports. Additionally, they gained 15.5 per cent from Japan and 0.8 per cent from France, indicating their ability to capture market shares from these countries.

On the other hand, they faced losses in their market shares to specific countries. Notably, they lost 6.9 per cent, 3.0 per cent, 21.0 per cent, 1.9 per cent, and 1.2 per cent of their shares to the Netherlands, Thailand, the USA, France and the UK, respectively.

Netherlands retained its 6.0 per cent shares. It gained 82.4, 49.3, 37.5, 7.4, and 6.9 per cent shares from UK, USA, France, China and Other countries, respectively. It lost 65.9, 21.8, and 6.2 per cent shares to France, USA and Japan, respectively. USA retained its 5.1 per cent shares. It gained its share of 45.9, 21.8, 21.0, 17.6, and 7.2 per cent from Thailand, Netherlands, Others, UK, and France, respectively. It lost 49.3, 32.4, and 8.1 per cent shares to Netherlands, China and Japan, respectively. France retained its 1.3 per cent share. It gained 65.9, and 39.0 per cent shares from Netherlands and Japan, respectively. It lost its major share of 37.5, 28.3 and 10.8 per cent to Netherlands, China, and Thailand, respectively.

Furthermore, Japan retained 36.8 per cent of its import share while, Thailand and UK retained none of its import share. Japan gained 8.1, 6.2 and 1.9 per cent of its share from USA, Netherlands, and France, respectively. It lost 39.0, 15.5 and 7.9 per cent of its share to France, Others and UK, respectively. Similarly, Thailand gained 19.3 per cent import share collectively from China, France and Others. It lost its total 100 per cent share to China and USA. Moreover, UK meagrely gained any import share but lost its 100 per cent share collectively to Netherlands and USA. The results showed that in quantity terms China, France and Japan were the stable markets and Thailand and UK were the unstable markets. The probable reason may be that these countries are importing castor oil from other regions.

In value terms, China was the largest importer of Indian castor. It retained about 74.3 per cent share of Indian castor oil during the entire study period. The probable reason behind this may be because of its increased domestic demand for Sebacic acid. This chemical constituent is used as monomer for nylon, cosmetics, plasticizers and lubricants. Furthermore, China gained 46.4 per cent share from other countries, 27.3 per cent share from Thailand, and 26.3 per cent share from France. Also it lost its 7.5, 6.6, 5.3, 4.9 and 1.3 per cent share to Others, Netherlands, USA, Thailand and UK, respectively. Netherlands and France also retained its 60.2 and 47.6 per cent import shares, respectively (Table 8 and Figure 6).

Table 8: Direction of castor oil export in value from India (2005 to 2019)

Country	China	Netherlands	USA	France	Japan	Thailand	UK	Others
China	**0.743**	0.066	0.053	0.000	0.000	0.049	0.013	0.075
Netherlands	0.000	**0.602**	0.000	0.371	0.020	0.000	0.000	0.007
USA	0.000	0.354	**0.311**	0.000	0.119	0.000	0.015	0.201
France	0.263	0.013	0.101	**0.476**	0.000	0.125	0.000	0.022
Japan	0.000	0.000	0.000	0.325	**0.415**	0.000	0.083	0.177
Thailand	0.273	0.000	0.514	0.000	0.000	**0.000**	0.092	0.120
UK	0.000	0.000	1.000	0.000	0.000	0.000	**0.000**	0.000
Others	0.464	0.000	0.025	0.000	0.016	0.010	0.023	**0.463**

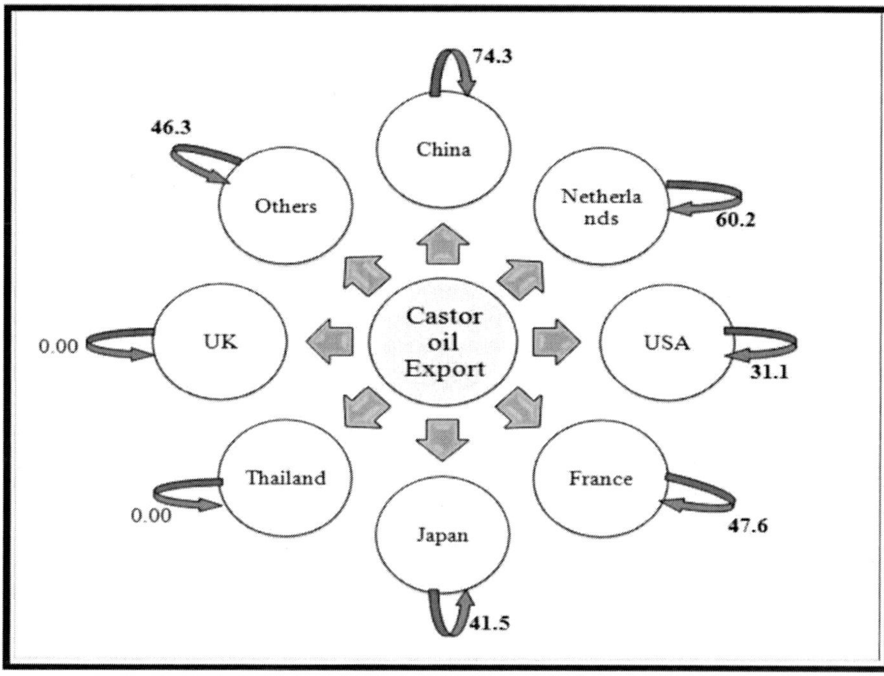

Fig. 6: Import shares of castor oil retained by major competing countries (Value)

Thailand and UK retained negligible per cent of import shares. Thailand lost majority share of 51.4 per cent and 27.3 per cent to USA and China, respectively. Similarly, UK lost its 100 per cent share to USA. Japan gained 11.9 and 2.0 per cent shares from USA and Netherlands, respectively. It lost its 32.5 and 17.7 per cent shares to France and other countries group, respectively. The results indicated that in value terms China, Netherlands and France are the stable markets and Thailand and UK were the unstable markets. Furthermore, USA was the emerging market for future prospects. These findings are in line with past researcher of Mandan (2019), Lokesh *et al.* (2020). They found that China was the most stable market followed by USA. Other countries *i.e.*, USA, France and Japan recorded a moderate level of retention per cent.

Conclusion

During entire study period, China emerged as the major importer of castor oil. About 42.59 per cent of quantity is exported to China, followed by Netherlands (15.89 per cent), USA (10.42 per cent), France (10.23 per cent) and Japan (2.80 per cent). China retained 74.6 per cent of Indian castor export, followed by other countries group that retained 66.1 per cent and Japan (36.8 per cent). Thailand and UK retained none of its import share. China was the largest importer of Indian castor. It retained 74.3 per cent share of Indian castor oil. Netherlands and France also retained its 60.2 and 47.6 per cent import shares, respectively. Study also concluded that the farmers involved in export of castor oil should focus on emerging countries like USA and France. These countries are providing better price and are reliable markets. Also China markets hold major share, so strategies should be used to hold the current market share of this country.

References

Cuddy, J. D., & Valle, P. D. (1978). Measuring the instability of time series data. Oxford bulletin of economics and statistics, 40 (1), 79-85.

Gondalia, V. K., Macwan, J. & Jadav, K. S. (2020). Emerging trends in export of groundnut, sesame and castor from India (1st ed.). Anand, Gujarat: Asian Printery.

Lokesh, G. B., Dandoti, K. & Wali, V. B. (2020). Trends in the direction of trade of castor oil exports from India. Indian Journal of Economics and Development, 16 (3), 381-388.

Mandan, M. B. (2019). Export performance of castor oil from India. AGRES - An International e-Journal, 8 (3), 199-204.

Rai, S. K., Charak, D. & Bharat, R. (2016). Scenario of oilseed crops across the globe. Plant Archives, 16 (1), 125-132.

Shanker, G. P. (2013). Export potential of castor (ricinus communis l.) Value added products in India (Master's Thesis, Acharya N G Ranga Agricultural University, Hyderabad, India)

Website Referred

www.castoroil.in
https://aps.dac.gov.in/APY/Public_Report1.aspx
www.castoroil.in/extraction/extraction.html
www.faostat.com
http://www.fao.org/faostat/en/#data/QC/visualize
https://eands.dacnet.nic.in/APY_96_To_06.htm
https://aps.dac.gov.in/APY/Public_Report1.aspx

5

Trend, Status & Government Initiatives to Promote Agri-Export

***Supriya*[1], *Aditya Bhooshan Srivastava*[2], *Pradeep Mishra*[2] *Prateek Kumar*[1] and *Mahima Priyanka Neerugatti*[1]**

[1]*Acharya Narendra Deva University of Agriculture & Technology Kumarganj, Ayodhya-224229, Uttar Pradesh*
[2]*College of Agriculture, Rewa, Jawaharlal Nehru Krishi Vishwa Vidyalaya Jabalpur-482004, Madhya Pradesh*

Abstract

India's agriculture sector plays a critical role in economic development, offering employment to a significant rural population and contributing notably to GDP. Despite limited natural resources, India is among the world's top producers of various crops and livestock. However, post-harvest losses, infrastructure gaps, and limited value addition hamper its full export potential. In recent years, agricultural exports have surge, with rice, spices, sugar, buffalo meat, and marine products emerging as key contributor. India has also expanded its export footprints across major global markets, including the USA, China, Bangladesh, and the UAE. Recognizing the strategic importance of agri-exports for economic growth, employment generation, and rural development, the government has launched initiatives such as the Agriculture Export Policy (AEP), Agri Export Zones (AEZs), and Market Access Initiatives (MAI). These measures aim to boost market access, infrastructure, and competitiveness. The integration of e-NAM, focus on quality standards, branding through Geographical Indications (GI), and establishment of Agri-Cells in key countries further support India's goal of becoming a global agri-export powerhouse. This work underscores the importance of a coherent export strategy to enhance farmer income, promote sustainable practices, and position India as a key player in the global agricultural value chain.

Keywords: *Agri-Export Policy (AEP), Agricultural Export Trends, Market Access and Diversification, Value addition and Processing*

Introduction

India's agriculture sector plays a pivotal role in its economy, benefiting from its vast and diverse landscape, favourable climate, and rich agricultural heritage. It encompasses a wide array of crops, livestock, and fisheries, contributing significantly to the Gross Domestic Product (GDP) and providing employment to around 58% of the population, particularly in rural areas. Despite having limited land and water resources (2.4% and 4% of the world's total, respectively), India supports a staggering 17.84% of the global population and 15% of the world's livestock. This emphasizes the need for continuous efforts to boost productivity, improve pre and post-harvest management, enhance processing capabilities, add value to agricultural products, and integrate technology and infrastructure in the agricultural sector (Sharma, 2021).

However, challenges persist in terms of productivity and post-harvest losses, with studies showing significant losses (ranging from 8% to 18%) in fresh fruits, vegetables, and fisheries due to deprived post-harvest management, and inadequate cold chain amenities. To address these issues, promoting agro-processing and agricultural exports is crucial, and India has made progress in this regard. As of 2019, India ranks tenth globally in agricultural exports, with its share increasing from 1.7% to 2.1% in recent years. India stands as one of the major producers of various agricultural and food output. In recent years, the country has experienced growth in its agriculture sector, with estimated growth rates of 3.00% in 2021-22 and 3.50% in 2022-23. It produces a wide range of crops, including jute, wheat, oilseeds, rice,pulses, sugarcane, tea, groundnuts, dairy products, tobacco and fruits. Notably, during 2021-22, India's tea output reached 1,344.40 million kg, and coffee output increased by 2.39percent year on year, reaching 3,420 lakh tonnes (FAO, 2021).

Additionally, the output of oilseeds intersected an assessed 37.15 million tonnes, and other products like rice, maize, mustard,wheat,pulses,and sugarcane attained record-high production levels during the same period. The states of Assam, Uttar Pradesh,Madhya Pradesh, Punjab, Gujarat, Haryana, West Bengal, Chhattisgarh,Andhra Pradeshand Karnataka stand as the top crop-producing regions in India. Major wheat production comes from Haryana, Punjab, Uttar Pradesh, Madhya Pradesh, Gujarat,Bihar, andRajasthan. Uttar Pradesh leads in sugarcane production, contributing about 48.00 % of the total, followed by Karnataka (9.00%) and Maharashtra (23.00 %) (GOI, 2021).

Importance of Agri-Exports for the Indian Economy

Agri-exports play avital role in shaping the Indian economic landscape and are of strategic importance for several reasons:

Economic Growth: Agriculture exports contribute substantially to India's economic growth. By selling agricultural products to other countries, India earns foreign exchange, which is essential for importing goods and services, strengthening its foreign reserves, and stabilizing the balance of trade.

Employment Generation: Agriculture employs a vast workforce in India. When agricultural products are exported, it stimulates the entire value chain, from farmers to agri-processors, traders, and exporters. This generates employment opportunities, especially in rural areas where job opportunities may be limited.

Rural Development: A significant proportion of India's population resides in rural areas and is directly dependent on agriculture. By promoting agri-exports, the income of farmers and rural communities can improve, leading to enhanced living standards, better infrastructure, and increased investments in rural development projects.

Diversification of Markets: Agri-exports open up new markets for Indian agricultural products. By reaching consumers worldwide, India can reduce its dependence on a single market and mitigate the risks associated with fluctuations in domestic demand or market conditions.

Value Addition and Processing: To meet international standards and cater to the preferences of foreign consumers, agri-exports often require value addition and processing. This encourages investment in processing industries, leading to higher value realization for farmers and a more significant contribution to the economy.

Global Competitiveness: Engaging in agri-export requires Indian farmers and exporters to adopt modern agricultural practices, adhere to quality standards, and maintain competitive prices. This fosters a culture of innovation and global competitiveness in the agricultural sector.

Foreign Policy and Diplomacy: Agriculture trade plays aessential role in India's foreign policy. It enhances diplomatic relations with other nations and facilitates engagement in various multilateral forums and international organizations related to agriculture and trade.

Food Security: While the primary focus of agri-exports is generating revenue, surplus production can also act as a buffer during periods of domestic food shortages. However, striking a balance between exports and ensuring domestic food security remains a challenge.

Objective and Vision

India, a vibrant nation with a population of 1.3 billion and rising disposable incomes has emerged as a significant consumer market and a crucial food product supplier. To bolster the "Make in India" initiative, there is a call for "Bake in India," emphasizing value-adding and processed agricultural goods. As the global population grows and farmlands diminish, India faces the challenge of growing sustainably, trading abundantly, and progressing harmoniously. To achieve the vision of doubling up farmer income, interventions are necessary to enhance productivity, price realization, and cost-efficiency in agriculture (GOI, 2021).

A dedicated agricultural export policy is much needed due to the federal structure of the Indian government, with different departments focusing on various aspects of agriculture. The Agriculture Export Policy must invigorate the entire value chain, encompassing export-oriented farm production, processing, transportation, infrastructure, and market access. The policy should align with existing agricultural frameworks and surplus agricultural produce. A symbiotic relationship exists between sustainable agriculture and a viable Agriculture Export Policy, as the latter aims to deliver improved incomes for farmers through export opportunities. By adopting a "Farmers' Centric Approach," the policy can focus on value addition at the source to minimize losses across the value chain and achieve food security while making India a prominent agriculture exporter globally. Additionally, the policy will promote food processing and manufacturing, elevating India share of value-added processed products in the global agriculture export market. The broad objectives and vision is highlighted below.

Objectives

The key strategies for enhancing India's agricultural exports are as follows:

Diversification: We aim to broaden our export range and target various destinations to increase the export of high-value and value-added farming products, with a particular focus on perishables.

Promotion of Non-Traditional Agri Products: We will actively endorse the export of traditional, unique, organic,ethnic, indigenous, and non-traditional agricultural products to expand our market presence.

Market Access: We will establish a dedicated institutional mechanism to pursue better market access, address trade barriers, and effectively handle sanitary and phytosanitary issues.

Global Integration: Our goal is to significantly enhance India's global agricultural exports by assimilating into the universal value chain at the earliest opportunity.

Farmer's Welfare: We are committed to empowering farmers by enabling them to seize export opportunities in overseas markets, leading to their economic betterment. These strategies aim to revitalize India's agricultural export sector and pave the way for sustainable growth and increased international market participation

Vision

"*Harness export potential of Indian agriculture, through suitable policy instruments, to make India global power in agriculture and raise farmer's income*".

Current scenario of IndianAgri export and import from the top 25 countries

The table presents a ranking of the top 25 countries based on their trade relations with India. It provides valuable information on the export and import values, total trade, and trade balance for each country. The United States holds the top position as India's largest trading partner, with a significant total trade value of US$ 10.33 trillion. China follows closely but with a substantial trade deficit, indicating that India imports more from China than it exports to the country.

The table also lists other significant trading partners of India, such as Indonesia, Iraq, Singapore, Hong Kong, South Korea, the Netherlands, Germany, Australia, Japan, the United Kingdom, Malaysia, South Africa, Qatar, Belgium, Switzerland, Thailand, Brazil, Vietnam, Italy, and Bangladesh (World Bank, 2021). The trade balance column indicates the trade surpluses and deficits between India and the respective countries. A positive trade balance indicates a surplus (exports exceed imports), while a negative trade balance indicates a deficit (imports exceed exports). In total, the top 25 countries account for a significant portion of India's trade, representing 67.93% of India's exports, 81.52% of India's imports, and 76.26% of India's total trade. However, when considering the trade balance, India has an overall trade deficit of US$ 21,13,327.41 with all countries in the table combined. These countries play essential roles in India's trade landscape, contributing to the country's overall trade volume and shaping its economic relations with the world. The trade balance column reveals the varying degrees of trade surpluses and deficits between India and the respective countries, providing insights into their trade competitiveness.

Country-wiseexport and import from India(2022-23)

Rank	Country	Export	Import	Total Trade	Trade Balance
1	U S A	6,30,152.54	4,03,494.87	10,33,647.41	2,26,657.68
2	China P RP	1,22,773.99	7,90,931.82	9,13,705.81	-6,68,157.83
3	U Arab Emts	2,53,852.38	4,27,406.56	6,81,258.94	-1,73,554.18
4	Saudi Arab	86,271.37	3,37,571.87	4,23,843.24	-2,51,300.50
5	Russia	25,462.70	3,74,003.31	3,99,466.00	-3,48,540.61
6	Indonesia	80,335.18	2,30,815.28	3,11,150.47	-1,50,480.10
7	Iraq	21,776.64	2,75,202.15	2,96,978.79	-2,53,425.50
8	Singapore	96,184.96	1,89,828.25	2,86,013.21	-93,643.29
9	Hong Kong	79,497.42	1,46,586.43	2,26,083.85	-67,089.01
10	Korea RP	53,275.35	1,70,631.81	2,23,907.15	-1,17,356.46
11	Netherland	1,74,409.18	47,877.24	2,22,286.42	1,26,531.95
12	Germany	81,396.91	1,28,033.42	2,09,430.33	-46,636.52
13	Australia	55,554.83	1,52,002.82	2,07,557.65	-96,447.99
14	Japan	43,834.30	1,32,614.78	1,76,449.08	-88,780.47
15	U K	91,719.95	71,824.53	1,63,544.48	19,895.42
16	Malaysia	57,265.17	1,02,185.23	1,59,450.40	-44,920.07
17	South Africa	67,873.23	83,117.53	1,50,990.76	-15,244.30
18	Qatar	15,801.00	1,35,017.80	1,50,818.80	-1,19,216.79
19	Belgium	70,998.03	73,585.19	1,44,583.22	-2,587.15
20	Switzerland	10,813.04	1,26,757.50	1,37,570.54	-1,15,944.46
21	Thailand	45,810.07	89,748.07	1,35,558.14	-43,938.01
22	Brazil	79,606.84	53,779.62	1,33,386.46	25,827.22
23	Vietnam Soc Rep	47,543.43	70,616.44	1,18,159.87	-23,073.01
24	Italy	69,762.87	44,680.06	1,14,442.94	25,082.81
25	Bangladesh PR	97,686.35	16,245.26	1,13,931.61	81,441.09
Total of Top 25 countries		*24,59,657.74*	*46,74,557.82*	*71,34,215.57*	*-22,14,900.08*
India's Total		**36,20,630.94**	**57,33,958.34**	**93,54,527.79**	**-21,13,327.41**
% Share of Top 25 countries		*67.93*	*81.52*	*76.26*	*104.81*

Source: World Bank, 2022

India stands as one of the world's major agricultural product exporters, with remarkable growth in its agricultural exports. In the period of April to December 2022, the export value of agricultural products surged from US$ 17.5 billion to US$ 19.7 billion, marking a notable increase compared to the same retro in the preceding fiscal year. The total agriculture exports for 2021-22 reached an impressive US$ 50.2 billion, displaying a significant 20% rise from US$ 41.3 billion in 2020-21.

The exportation of agri and allied goods, marine goods, plantation goods, and textile and allied goods are the primary areas of concentration for India's agricultural sector. Exports of agricultural and related goods had a value of $37.3 billion in US dollars and experienced a healthy growth rate of 17% over the course of 2020-21. Rice is the most important agricultural product exported from India, accounting for more than 19% of the country's overall export of agricultural goods throughout the years 2021-22. Other important exports include spices, sugar, and buffalo meat, each of which contributed 9 percent, 8 percent, and 7 percent respectively to the total value of agricultural exports in the years 2021-22.

The growth of agriculture exports extends to wheat as well, with its exports reaching US$ 2.1 billion in 2021-22, showing significant expansion from US$ 568 million in 2020-21. Coffee exports also witnessed a jump of 1.66%, reaching 4 lakh tonnes in 2022, attributed to increased exports of instant coffee and re-exports. The sophisticated exports of marine products, amounting to US$ 7.7 billion, have been beneficial for farmers in coastal states likeOdisha, Gujarat,West Bengal,Andhra Pradesh, Tamil Nadu,Kerala, and Maharashtra. The government's commitment to increasing farmers' income is evident in its efforts to boost agriculture exports (APEDA, 2021)

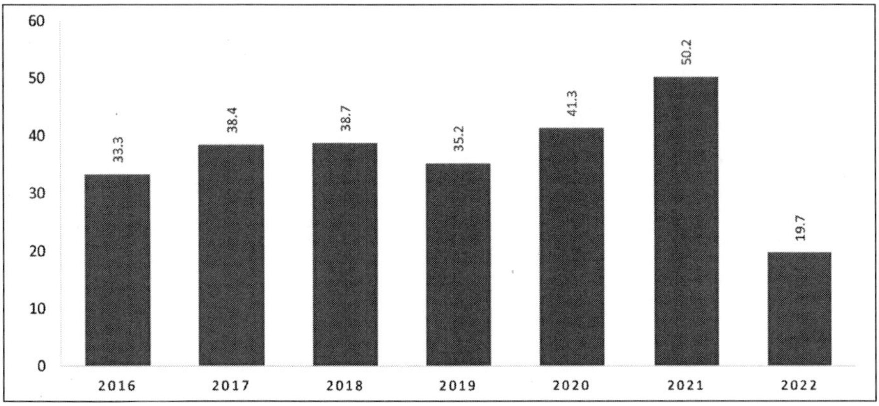

Fig. 1: India agri-export trend (US$billion)
Source:APEDA, 2021

The expansion of exports has been facilitated by a number of various activities that have been carried out under the auspices of APEDA. These activities include the staging of B2B exhibits in a variety of countries as well as the investigation of new potential markets by means of product-specific and general marketing campaigns. In addition, the government has recognized 220 laboratories as being able to provide testing services for a wide variety of items, which would benefit exporters from all over India. They have also identified 50 agricultural products that have a significant potential for export. These measures have played a pivotal role in driving India's agriculture sector to new heights in the global market.

Export Destination

India's agricultural products find significant demand in various countries, with Indonesia, UAE,Bangladesh, Nepal, Vietnam, Malaysia, and USA being the largest importers. Other importing nations include Egypt, China,Iraq, and Iran. In the fiscal year 2021-22, Bangladesh emerged as the top distributor of Indian agricultural goods, accounting for US$ 2.83 billion and holding an 11.46% share of the total exports. Bangladesh primarily imports agri& allied products, amounting to US$ 3.8 billion, while U.A.E stands as the second-largest importer with US$ 2.3 billion worth of imports. Notably, China and the United States are the most important markets for India's maritime industry.

The Indian government regularly arranges virtual-buyer seller meetings (V-BSMs) with major importing nations globally in order to promote geographical indications (GI) associated with agricultural and processed food goods in India. Thus far, 17 V-BSMs have successfully taken place with countries such as Iran,Indonesia, Belgium,Kuwait, andSwitzerland. Similar initiatives have been carried out for Canada (organic products), the United Arab Emirates (GI products), and the United States (GI products), as well as for Qatar, Thailand, Australia, Bhutan, Oman, Azerbaijan, South Africa, and Germany. In order to enhance Indian exports to specific destinations and bolster trade, tourism, technology, and investment objectives, the government has established thirteen Agri-Cells in Indian embassies located in Bangladesh, Argentina,Nepal, Vietnam, Indonesia, Malaysia, USA,Japan,Saudi Arabia, China, Singapore and UAE. These Agri-Cells serve to provide real-time inputs and support, ensuring the improvement of Indian exports to these countries.

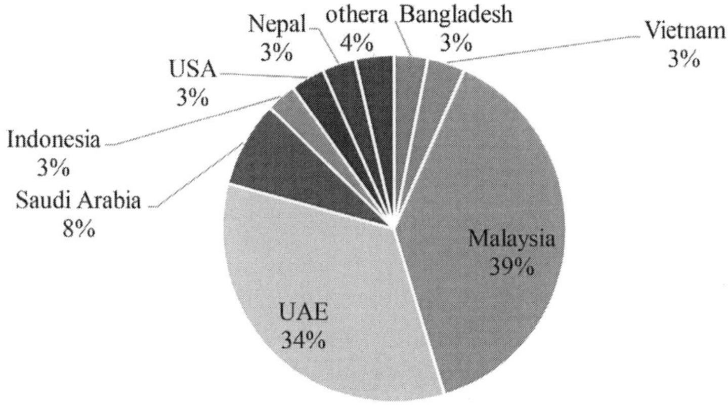

Fig. 2: Country Wise approximate Share of export (2021-22)
Source: *World trade Organization,2021*

Government Initiative

The Indian government has taken several initiatives to promote and boost agricultural exports from the country. These initiatives are aimed at enhancing market access, increasing competitiveness, improving infrastructure, and providing support to farmers and exporters. Some of the key government initiatives for India's agri-export are:

1. **Agriculture Export Policy (AEP):**In order to establish a framework for fostering agricultural exports, the government unveiled the Agriculture Export Policy in 2018. The policy aims to double farmers' income by promoting exports of agricultural products and processed foods. It focuses on enhancing export-oriented production, improving infrastructure, and facilitating market access for Indian products in international markets.
2. **Market Access Initiative (MAI) Scheme**: This scheme provides monetary assistance to Indian exporters and Agricultural and Processed Food Products Export Development Authority (APEDA) to promote Indian agricultural products in foreign markets. It supports participation in international trade fairs, exhibitions, buyer-seller meets, and other promotional activities.
3. **Agri Export Zones (AEZs):** The government has identified specific geographical regions with the potential to excel in the production and export of certain agricultural products. These regions are designated as Agri Export Zones and are provided with necessary infrastructure, technology, and support to boost their export capabilities. Export Promotion Schemes: Various export promotion schemes like the

Merchandise Export from India Scheme (MEIS) and the Service Export from India Scheme (SEIS) provide incentives and benefits to exporters, including those engaged in agricultural exports.

4. **Quality Control and Standards**: The government emphasizes maintaining high-quality standards for agricultural products to enhance their competitiveness in international markets. Certification and accreditation programs are encouraged to ensure compliance with international quality and safety standards.
5. **Branding and Geographical Indications (GI):** The government supports the promotion of Indian agricultural products through branding and obtaining Geographical Indications (GI) certifications. GI tags help protect the unique identity and reputation of products specific to certain regions, boosting their market value and recognition.
6. **Infrastructure Development:** The government invests in developing modern infrastructure, such as cold chains, storage facilities, and processing units, to decrease post-harvest losses and boost the shelf life of perishable agricultural products.
7. **E-NAM (National Agriculture Market):** E-NAM is an online platform that integrates agricultural produce markets across the country. It facilitates efficient price discovery and enables farmers to access a larger market, thus promoting agricultural exports.
8. **Research and Development:** The government supports research and development in agriculture, including improved seeds, crop varieties, and technology adoption, to enhance productivity and competitiveness. These initiatives collectively aim to empower Indian farmers and agribusinesses to tap into global markets, increase the value of agricultural exports, and contribute to the growth of India's agri-export sector.

Conclusion

India's Agriculture Export Policy stands as a pivotal instrument in realizing the country's vision of becoming a prominent player in the global agri-export market. This policy outlines a comprehensive framework that aims to enhance agricultural productivity, improve post-harvest management, and strengthen infrastructure for efficient export operations. By fostering an enabling environment for farmers, exporters, and agribusinesses, the policy strives to double farmers' income while promoting sustainable agricultural practices.

Through strategic initiatives like Market Access Initiative (MAI) Scheme, Agri Export Zones (AEZs), and various export promotion schemes, the government has taken proactive measures to facilitate market entry and boost the competitiveness of Indian agricultural products in international markets. The emphasis on quality control, branding, and obtaining Geographical Indications (GI) certifications further enhances the market value and global recognition of India's unique agricultural produce.

Moreover, the establishment of Agri-Cells in key countries and the organization of virtual buyer-seller meets (V-BSMs) demonstrate the government's commitment to providing real-time support and fostering international trade partnerships.

As India continues to evolve into a dynamic force in the global agricultural arena, the successful execution of the Agriculture Export Policy will be crucial in unlocking the immense potential of India's agricultural sector. By harmonizing sustainable agricultural practices with efficient trade strategies, India is well-positioned to not only augment its export revenue but also contribute significantly to global food security. With its diverse agricultural heritage, favourable climate conditions, and the government's unwavering commitment, India is poised to emerge as a key player in the realm of agri-export, contributing to the prosperity of its farmers, agribusinesses, and the overall economy.

References

Agricultural and Processed Food Products Export Development Authority (APEDA). (2021). Official Website. Retrieved from https://apeda.gov.in/

Food and Agriculture Organization (FAO). (2021). India - Country Profile. Retrieved from http://www.fao.org/india/fao-in-india/india-country-profile/en/

GOI, 2021. Ministry of Commerce and industry, Department of Commerce. Retrieved from https://commerce.gov.in/

Sharma, V. (2021). Agricultural Sector in India: Challenges and Opportunities. Journal of Economics and Sustainable Development, 12(13), 99-108.

World Bank. (2022). World Integrated Trade Solution (WITS). Retrieved from https://wits.worldbank.org/

World Trade Organization (WTO). (2022). World Trade Statistical Review. Retrieved from https://www.wto.org/

6

Augmentation of Agri-exports in India Through Intervention of APEDA

Souvik Ghosh, Siddhesh Zade and Apoorva Veldandi

National Dairy Research Institute, Karnal, Haryana

ABSTRACT

India's agricultural exports play a pivotal role in driving economic growth, enhancing rural livelihoods, and generating employment. The Agricultural and Processed Food Products Export Development (APEDA), established under the Ministry of Commerce and Industry, has significantly contributed to the augmentation of India's agri-exports through strategic interventions. This chapter explores APEDA's multifaceted initiatives, including quality control, infrastructure development, product diversification, and digital innovations such as paperless systesm, mobile apps, and virtual trade fairs. Notable efforts include the promotion of Geographical Indication (GI) products, expansion of Agri-Export Zones (AEZs), and international marketing of millets during the International Year of Millets (IYOM 2023). APEDA's Market Access Initiative (MAI) and Agri-Exchange portal have facilitated global trade linkages, while collaborations with institutions and FPOs have strengthened grassroots connections. Recent achievements include surpassing USD 19.69 billion in agri-export value in 2022-23 and expanding to over 200 countries. This comprehensive engagement reflects APEDA's central role in branding Indian agriculture on the global stage and positioning India as a reliable exporter of high-quality food products.

Keywords: *APEDA, Geographical Indications (GI), Market Access Initiative (MAI), Virtual Trade Fair and International Year of Millets (IYOM)*

Introduction

Agricultural exports are important to a country's economy since they contribute to foreign exchange profits, create job opportunities, and improve rural livelihoods. The Indian agrarian economy provides considerable service to the world food basket. Indian dishes, spices, snacks, fruits, and vegetables are highly known for their high quality all over the world. India is the world's leading producer of milk, animal products, pulses, bananas, mangoes, guava, veggies, and so on. As a leader in different agricultural categories, its contribution through exports reaches more than 100 nations worldwide. The initial segment of the fiscal year 2022-23 (April-September) witnessed a noteworthy uptick of 25% in the agricultural and processed food product exports, as contrasted with the corresponding period in FY 2021-22. The initial data, as released through the Directorate General of Statistics and Commercial Intelligence (DGCI&S), demonstrates a comprehensive surge of 25% in the value of agricultural and processed food exports in USD, spanning from April to September 2022. In light of these developments, (APEDA) plays the duty of paramount importance, as it actively contributes to the facilitation and enhancement of agricultural export endeavors.

About APEDA

Establishment: The Agricultural and Processed Food Products Export Development Authority (APEDA) was instituted by the Government of India in accordance with the APEDA Act, a legislation endorsed by the Parliament in December of 1985. According to a notification published in the Extraordinary: Part-II [Sec. 3(ii): 13.2.1986] of the Gazette of India, this Act (2 of 1986) became operative on February 13, 1986. Notably, India recently commemorated the 37th anniversary of its founding on February 13, 2023. This Authority was established as a replacement for the Processed Food Export Promotion Council (PFEPC). It operates within the jurisdiction of the Indian government's Ministry of Commerce and Industry.

With its headquarters and sixteen regional offices, the company has been providing services to the agri-export industry throughout the country's agro-potential states.

- Head offices- New Delhi
- Regional offices-

Ahmedabad, Bengaluru, Bhopal, Chandigarh, Chennai, Guwahati, Jammu and Ladakh, Kochi, Kolkata, Mumbai, Srinagar, Telangana, Tripura, Varanasi, Visakhapatnam.

Current Chairman of APEDA - Shri Abhishek Dev, IAS

Current director of APEDA-Dr. Tarun Bajaj

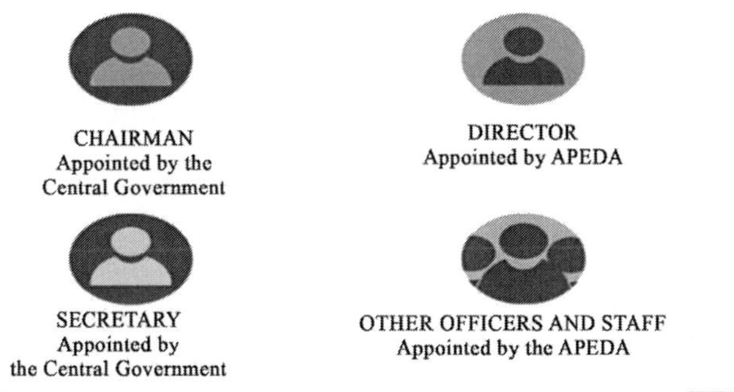

Fig. 1: Administrative set-up of APEDA in India

Functions of APEDA

a) **Product Development and Diversification:** APEDA identifies potentially exportable agricultural and processed food goods. It contributes to the development and diversification of these items, with a focus on enhancing their quality and marketability.

b) **Quality Control and Standardization:** Maintaining India's credibility in the global market requires ensuring that exported products fulfil international quality requirements. APEDA promotes quality standards and certifies products, increasing consumer confidence and opening opportunities to worldwide markets.

c) **Market Research and Promotion:** APEDA performs market research to discover worldwide industry trends, demands, and opportunities. Based on this study, it develops methods to promote Indian agricultural and processed food goods in foreign markets, thereby increasing their market reach.

d) **Infrastructure Development:** APEDA assists in the building of post-harvest infrastructure such as cold storage facilities, processing units, and packaging centres to facilitate agricultural product exports. This infrastructure development improves product preservation and quality while in transit.

e) **Capacity Building:** APEDA offers training and capacity-building programs for agricultural export stakeholders such as farmers, exporters, and processing units. This assists them in understanding international market demands and adhering to quality standards. The Basmati Export Development Foundation (BEDF) hosts various training programmes for human resource development among stakeholders throughout the country.

f) **Export Facilitation**: The authority supports exporters in getting various permits and certifications required for agricultural product exportation. It also examines trade-related issues and seeks to resolve them.

Products monitored by APEDA

- Vegetables, fruits, and their derivatives.
- Meat and Meat-Related Products.
- Poultry and Poultry-Related Products.
- Products made from milk.
- Bakery products, biscuits, and confectionery.
- Products made from honey, jaggery, and sugar.
- Cocoa and its derivatives, as well as various chocolates.
- Beverages, both alcoholic and non-alcoholic.
- Cereals and products made from cereals.
- Groundnuts, peanuts, and walnuts are all examples of nuts.
- Papads, chutneys and pickles are all options.
- Guar Gum.
- Floriculture and floral products.
- Plants used for herbal and medicinal purposes.
- Rice bran that has been de-oiled.
- A brined green pepper.
- Cashew Nuts and Their Byproducts

Rice variety of Basmati has been added to the APEDA Act's Second Schedule. It was bestowed with the task of controlling sugar imports.

Initiatives by APEDA

1. IT-enabled paperless working

APEDA, in its pursuit of enhancing the ease of conducting business and fostering the expansion of exports from India, has championed IT-driven operations. The overarching objective is to elevate the realm of agricultural product exports to unprecedented heights. To elevate administrative efficacy and potency, APEDA has embarked on a multifaceted approach encompassing paperless office procedures, incorporating re-engineering techniques, digital signatures, and electronic payment capabilities. Further enhancements include the implementation of the APEDA Mobile App, phased rollout of online services, meticulous monitoring and evaluation mechanisms, equitable access provisioning, and the creation of a virtual trade fair platform.

The virtual trade fair serves as a novel avenue wherein prospective buyers, importers, and curious onlookers can explore a diverse array of food products showcased by exporters. The distinct advantage lies in the seamless integration of interactive technology into the trading process, facilitating frictionless virtual interactions.

Underlining its commitment to innovation, APEDA debuted its pioneering Virtual Trade Fair (VTF) initiative from March 10th to March 12th, 2021. This landmark effort was conceived with the aim of bolstering India's potential export market for agricultural and processed food goods, particularly in the challenging landscape of the COVID-19 pandemic. The focal point of the fair, themed 'India Rice and Agro Commodity,' was to spotlight the export feasibility of an assortment of agricultural products.

The VTF showcased an array of vital commodities including Wheat, maize, groundnuts, coarse grains, millets, basmati and non-basmati rice. With participation from 135 exhibitors, the VTF garnered substantial attention. Notably, the event attracted the engagement of 266 customers spanning the globe, hailing from countries like the Philippines, Qatar, Sudan, Myanmar, the Netherlands, Afghanistan, Bahrain, Egypt, Fiji, the United Arab Emirates, Brazil, New Zealand, France, Saudi Arabia, the United Kingdom, and Peru. The strategic collaboration with Indian embassies worldwide played a pivotal role in drawing potential buyers to the event.

- **Mobile App developed by APEDA**

  1. APEDA RCAC for Basmati Rice: APEDA is authorized by the Foreign Trade Policy to register all contracts and issue Registration-cum-Allocation Certificates (RCAC) for the Basmati Rice export. This mobile app allows registered exporters to apply for the Basmati Rice RCAC. It will also make it easier for registered exporters/stakeholders to obtain e-services by simply filling out and uploading the necessary paperwork for the issuing of RCAC for Basmati Rice.
  2. Farm Registration: This tool allows farmers to apply for farm registration online and track the status of their applications.The mobile software also helps state horticulture departments record information about farmers, their farms, and their products, as well as farm inspections. For easy tracking I tracking menu along with exporter log-in option are available on APEDA`s Website.

Different individual webpages is build up by APEDA like GRAPE.NET for Grapes, ANAR.NET for Pomegranate, PEA-NUT.NET for Peanut , TRACENET for Organic products ,MEAT.NET for meat products and BASMATI.NET for Basmati rice. APEDA provides these internet-based electronic services to stakeholders by facilitating testing and certification of agricultural product to export from India. on the basis of discussions with exporters these IT services gathers, stores, and disseminates quality assurance information entered by participants in the Agri-produce industry along with forward and backward traces and food supply chain in India, such as exporters, laboratories, and PSC authorities.

APEDA conceived, developed, and launched the Millets Portal as part of the Indian Millets web promotion. To promote millets, it launched also an individual platform called Indian Millet Exchange.

2. Market Access Initiative (MAI)

This project provides financial help to exporters and export groups in order for them to participate in international trade fairs, exhibitions, and buyer-seller meetings. This aids in the development of business partnerships and the promotion of Indian products on a worldwide scale. APEDA has created a Market Intelligence Cell, and the process of distributing reports on E-market intelligence that contain in-depth market analysis has started.

3. Geographical Indications (GI) Tags

In alignment with Prime Minister Narendra Modi's encouragement for the promotion of local goods through "vocal for local" along with "Atmanirbhar Bharat" initiatives, APEDA has already placed significant emphasis on advancing the export prospects of regionally identified Geographical Indications (GI) labeled products, indigenous and culturally distinctive agrarian commodities. This strategic approach has led to the identification of novel product lines and export destinations, subsequently facilitating trial shipments.

At present, the tally stands at 417 registered GI products, with an impressive count of over 150 GI-designated agricultural and food items. Notably, More than one hundred of these GI products that are registered are included in the APEDA scheduled categories, which include cereals, fresh produce, vegetables, and processed foods.

India's diverse range of offerings includes ethnic and GI-labeled items such as Puffed rice, dried mahua flowers, jackfruit, jamun, dragon fruit, proprietary village rice, and Burmese grapes. Noteworthy among these are mango varieties boasting GI recognition, Bhalia wheat, King Chilli, Madurai malli, Mihidana, Sitabhog, Dahanu Gholvad Sapota, Vazhakulam pineapple, Marayoor jaggery, Jalgaon banana, as well as the esteemed Khasi Mandarin (GI) hailing from Meghalaya, to name but a few. These offerings are a testament to India's rich agricultural heritage and its commitment to fostering sustainable and culturally significant trade endeavors.

Farmer Connect Initiative

APEDA collaborates extensively with farmers to educate them on global market demands, quality standards, and best agricultural practices. This guarantees a consistent supply of high-quality produce for export. Additionally, APEDA has created a Farmer Connect Portal on its website to give FPOs and FPCs a platform. and Cooperatives to communicate with exporters.

4. Agri-Export Zones (AEZs)

APEDA targets certain geographic areas with the ability to produce a specific export product of interest. It then promotes the establishment of Agri-Export Zones, which focus on increasing production practices, quality, and post-harvest management in order to increase exports from such areas.

In close cooperation with the Ministry of Commerce and Industry, APEDA has orchestrated a remarkable transformation of landlocked Purvanchal into a burgeoning hub for agricultural exports. This feat was achieved through the expeditious establishment of the Varanasi Agro-Export Hub (VAEH). In the wake of this initiative, the Varanasi region, previously constrained by insufficient infrastructure leading to minimal export undertakings, has now become a vibrant center of agricultural export activities.

With APEDA's pivotal role, the Varanasi region has witnessed a remarkable shift in its export landscape, achieving noteworthy milestones in an impressively short span of time. The introduction of unprecedented accomplishments from the Purvanchal region has reshaped the export scenario. Particularly noteworthy is the achievement of facilitating agri exports from the Himalayan belt spanning Jammu and Kashmir to Ladakh, which stands as a monumental advancement in the region's agricultural export journey.

The impact of this initiative extends beyond the Varanasi region. Landlocked states like the Madhya Pradesh, Uttar Pradesh, Uttaranchal, Bihar, and the North Eastern Region have witnessed a significant boost in their agricultural exports. This transformation has been achieved by efficiently sourcing products from local farmers and seamlessly integrating them into the retail chains of importing nations. The result has been an upliftment of the agricultural export sector across these states, marking a substantial contribution to India's overall agricultural trade.

5. Organic Product Certification

With the growing global demand for organic products, APEDA has carried out a significant role in promoting organic farming and gaining organic certifications. This has aided the recognition and acceptability of local organic products in global markets. It serves as the National Accreditation Board's (NAB) secretariat for the accreditation of Certification Bodies for organic exports under the National Programme for Organic Production (NPOP). "Organic Products" for export can only be certified if they are being produced, value added as well as packaged in accordance with the requirements outlined in the file "National Programme for Organic Production (NPOP)."

Recent Achievements of APEDA in Trade

- Through its active involvement, APEDA has propelled agricultural product exports to an unprecedented pinnacle, reaching a notable 19.69 billion of USD from April to December 2022-23, concurrently broadening the spectrum of exports to span over two hundred countries.
- In the fiscal year 2021-22, APEDA accomplished the export of agricultural products valued at USD 24.77 billion.
- The current fiscal year's (2022-23) objective for APEDA stands at USD 23.56 billion. Remarkably, as of December 20, 2022, the organization has realized 84% of this target, amounting to USD 19.69 billion. With the remaining portion of the goal projected to be fulfilled within the stipulated timeframe.

Table 1: Share of various agricultural commodities in total export of APEDA

Products		April - June	(2023-24)		Unit value	% Change		% Share in APEDA's total Export	
		QTY	VALUE		(In USD	Rs.	USD	Rs.	USD
		In MTs	Rs. Crores	USD Million	Per Tonnes)				
Schedule Products									
A. Floriculture		4784	171	21	4339	-17.73	-22.75	0.33	0.33
B. Fruit & Vegetable Seeds		4187	308	37	8957	26.58	19.01	0.59	0.59
Floriculture & Seeds			479	58		6.20	-0.21	0.92	0.92
A. Fresh Fruits		337627	2221	270	801	34.01	25.38	4.27	4.28
B. Fresh Vegetables		929875	1681	205	220	12.63	5.70	3.24	3.24
Fruits & Vegetables			3902	475		23.88	16.08	7.51	7.51
A. Pulses		191843	1641	200	1041	4.62	-1.52	3.16	3.16
B. Processed Vegetables		92572	1146	139	801	147.27	132.42	4.27	4.28
C. Processed Fruits & Juices		115924	1465	178	220	27.72	19.86	3.24	3.24
Livestock Products			4253	517		12.42	5.67	8.18	8.19
A	Buffalo Meat	289142	6814	829	2867	1.70	-4.50	13.11	13.11
B	Sheep/Goat Meat	3178	178	22	6805	27.08	19.13	0.34	0.34
C	Animal Casings	2545	58	7	2760	-47.46	-50.58	0.11	0.11
D	Processed Meat	45	2	0.3	5704	-37.59	-41.34	0.00	0.00
E	Other Meat	11	1	0.1	6506	-94.67	-95.03	0.00	0.00
F.	Poultry Product	NA	338	41		64.35	54.36	0.65	0.65
G.	Dairy Products	38831	911	111	2853	-38.11	-41.88	1.75	1.75
Processed Food And Vegetables			8301	1010		-3.94	-9.80	15.98	15.98

Products		April - June	(2023-24)		Unit value	% Change		% Share in APEDA's total Export	
		QTY	VALUE		(In USD	Rs.	USD	Rs.	USD
		In MTs	Rs. Crores	USD Million	Per Tonnes)				
A. Groundnuts		159746	1753	213	1335	54.74	45.15	3.37	3.37
B. Guargum		99076	944	115	1159	-35.25	-39.09	1.82	1.82
D. Cereal Preparations		121682	1607	195	1606	19.61	12.30	3.09	3.09
E. Cocoa Products		7191	284	35	4804	-8.05	-13.70	0.55	0.55
F. Milled Products		50559	231	28	556	-81.17	-82.30	0.45	0.45
G. Alcoholic Beverages		73541	775	94	1281	35.05	26.80	1.49	1.49
H. Misc. Processed Items		NA	3464	421		28.44	20.69	6.67	6.67
Other Processed Foods			9057	1102		3.62	-2.66	17.43	17.43
A	Basmati Rice	1172684	10673	1299	1107	19.27	12.17	20.54	20.54
B.	Non-Basmati Rice	4057662	12518	1523	375	3.54	-2.69	24.09	24.09
C.	Wheat	4387	11	1	292	-99.87	-99.88	0.02	0.02
D.	Other Cereals	880386	2071	252	286	-12.59	-17.76	3.99	3.99
Cereals			25273	3075		-20.22	-25.07	48.64	48.64
Total (Excluding Cashew)			51264	6237		-9.18	-14.71	98.66	98.66
A. Cashew Kernels		11809	680	83	7009	6.13	-0.49	1.31	1.31
B. Cashew Nut Shell Liquid		2293	14	2	769	-7.99	-13.58	0.03	0.03
Cashew			695	85		5.79	-0.81	1.34	1.34
Total (Including Cashew)			51959	6321		-9.01	-14.55	100.00	100.00

APEDA's Trade Fair Participation List for The Year 2023-24

1. BIOFACH 2023: 14th-17th February 2023, Nuremberg, Germany.
2. Gulfood 2023 Dubai, UAE, 20-24 February, 2023.
3. Natural Products Expo West: 07th to 11th March 2023, Anaheim Convention Center Anaheim, CA, USA
4. International Food and Drink (IFE) and BSM, London, UK (20th - 22nd March, 2023)
5. SIAL Food Canada and BSM, Canada (9th - 11th May, 2023)
6. Seoul Food & Hotel, Korea (30th May - 6th June, 2023)
7. Big Seven, Johannesburg, South Africa (18th - 20th June, 2023)
8. Summer Fancy Food Show, New York, US (25th - 27th June, 2023)
9. Food & Hotel Show, Jakarta, Indonesia (25th - 28th July, 2023)
10. Vietfood & Beverage, Ho Chi Minh, Vietnam (10th - 12th August, 2023)
11. Buyer Seller Meet and Road Shows, Indonesia (September, 2023)
12. Buyer Seller Meet and Road Shows, Japan (September, 2023)
13. Fine Food, Sydney, Australia (11th - 14th September, 2023)
14. World food Moscow 85 Buyer Seller Meet, Moscow, Russia (19th - 22nd September, 2023)
15. Anuga Food Fair, Germany (7th - 11th October, 2023)
16. Saudi Agro Food, Riyadh, Saudi Arabia (23rd - 26th October 2023)

Role of APEDA in IYOM 2023

The observance of International Year of Millets (IYoM) is driven by the intention of enhancing awareness about the nutritional and health advantages of millet consumption, especially in the context of challenging and fluctuating climatic conditions. This initiative further underscores the commitment to augmenting research and development efforts as well as extension services pertaining to millet cultivation. A vital facet of this endeavor is the promotion of Indian millets and value-added millet-based products on a global scale. To achieve this, APEDA has devised a strategy to amplify export promotion, marked by active participation in International Trade Fairs throughout 2023.

The largest B2B international hospitality and food event in Asia, the renowned AAHAR food display, APEDA unveiled an assorted range of millet products catering to all age groups, thoughtfully priced between Rs 5 and Rs 15. These millet products, meticulously developed by APEDA, boast the qualities of being gluten-free, natural, and patented.

This diverse assortment includes cream cookies, biscuits made with milk and salt, peanut butter made from ragi and jowar, jowar upma, pongal and khichadi, and several millet malts made from jowar, ragi, and bajra. A notable innovation also introduced by APEDA is the "Millet in Minutes" Ready-to-Eat (RTE) products, featuring options such as Noodles, Biryani, Pongal, Khichadi, Upma, and more. This innovation stands as a pioneering development in the food industry, catering to the fast-paced demands of the modern world while ensuring a health-conscious approach.

AAHAR, hosted at Pragati Maidan, was co-hosted by the India Trade Promotion Organization (ITPO) and APEDA. This exemplifies APEDA's commitment to fostering national and international events that bolster agri-export endeavors. A recent instance was, the New Delhi-based Global Millets (Shree Anna) Conference, aimed at promoting Indian millet exports and affording farmers access to diverse markets. The conference brought together more than 100 Indian millet exhibitors representing different parts of the nation, alongside participants from Kuwait, Italy, Germany, Vietnam, Kenya, Malawi, Bhutan, and Japan.

As part of its cooperative efforts, APEDA works with state agricultural institutions, the Indian Institute of Millets Research (IIMR), Hyderabad, has supported the incubation of more than 200 start-ups. These initiatives focus on creating an array of value-added millet-based products to enhance consumption.

Evidencing its dedication to global outreach, APEDA recently formalized a Memorandum of Understanding (MoU) signed on February 21, 2023, with Lulu Hypermarket LLC.This strategic collaboration is geared towards tapping into the possibility of millets being sent to the Gulf Cooperation Council (GCCs). With this, APEDA aspires to position millet products and value-added offerings prominently across international markets, leveraging the widespread reach of Lulu Group. Lulu Group, recognized for its retail hypermarket chain presence spanning nations such as Saudi Arabia, the United Arab Emirates, Egypt, India, Qatar, Bahrain, Kuwait, Oman, and the Far East, aligns seamlessly with APEDA's global promotion objectives.

Recent Activities Undertaken by APEDA

- APEDA, Ministry of Commerce and Industry, organized a Buyer Seller Meet to boost Dragon Fruit export.
- APEDA organizes agricultural demonstrations and farm training for students as part of the National Education Policy.

- APEDA sponsors an 8-day mango festival in Bahrain to increase mango exports.
- APEDA hosts an International Buyer Seller Meet in Leh to increase the export of apricots and other agricultural goods from the UT of Ladakh.
- It introduced gluten-free millet products for people of all ages at reasonable costs.
- APEDA co-organized the 36th edition of AAHAR 2022, which will take place from April 26th to 30th at Pragati Maidan.
- APEDA sponsored an 8-day mango festival in Bahrain to increase mango exports.
- APEDA hosts an International Buyer Seller Meet in Leh to increase the export of apricots and other agricultural goods from the UT of Ladakh.
- APEDA will co-organize the 36th edition of AAHAR 2022, which will take place from April 26th to 30th at Pragati Maida.
- APEDA has concluded an MOU with the National Research Development Corporation (NRDC).
- APEDA hosted a webinar for Indian exporters on new EU laws on organic products.
- APEDA conducted a meeting to enhance India's wheat exports in the midst of a historic increase in wheat shipments for the current fiscal year.
- APEDA held 75 awareness-and training-raising events in honor of Azadi Ka Amrit Mahotsav for farmers in seven states that cultivate Basmati rice.
- APEDA signs an agreement with the GB Pant University of Agriculture and Technology to boost Uttarakhand's agricultural exports.
- APEDA signs an agreement with the Central Citrus Research Institute (ICAR) in Nagpur to boost value-added products and citrus exports.
- In order to inform producers, exporters, state government representatives, and other interested parties about the potential for agricultural goods to be exported as well as the requirements for exports under the National Programme for Organic Production, APEDA has initiated a number of initiatives.
- The initial consignment of value-added goods made from nutmeg (jaiphal), passion fruit, and jackfruit from Kerala to Australia was flagged off by the APEDA.

- APEDA and ICAR—Indian Institute of Millet Research—signed Memorandums of Understanding to improve export possibilities and farmer income.
- APEDA, in conjunction with HPMC, sold five distinct apple cultivars to Bahrain.
- APEDA signed an agreement with the University of Agricultural Sciences in Bangalore to increase agri-exports.

Overall Contributions to Agri Exports

a) Economic Growth- Agricultural exports contribute considerably to India's economic growth by gaining foreign currency and increasing farmer and rural community income.

b) Employment Generation- In India, the agriculture sector employs a sizable number of people. APEDA indirectly contributes to job creation by boosting agricultural exports, both on the farm and in downstream sectors.

c) Market Diversification- The initiatives of APEDA have resulted in the diversification of India's export markets. This diversification lessens the country's reliance on a single market and aids in the management of risks associated with swings in demand.

d) Brand India- APEDA's quality standards and certifications improve the image of Indian agricultural and processed food goods in international markets, resulting in a greater global brand presence.

e) Technological Advancement- Exporters are encouraged to use innovative technology for production, processing, and packaging in order to satisfy worldwide standards. This results in agricultural technical breakthroughs.

f) Small and Medium Enterprises (SMEs) Empowerment- APEDA's assistance allows agricultural and food processing SMEs to reach the worldwide market. This helps their growth and competitiveness.

Conclusion

The Export Development Authority for Agricultural and Processed Food Products (APEDA) plays a significant role in facilitating agricultural exports from India. APEDA plays a critical role in boosting the global presence of Indian agricultural and processed food products through its various functions, initiatives, and contributions. However, as problems persist, ongoing collaboration among stakeholders, combined with smart investments, will be required to strengthen India's position in the global agri-export scene.

References

Apeda. (n.d.). APEDA press release.

Das, M. (2021). National Bank for Agriculture and Rural Development (NABARD). In International Journal of Research and Review (Vol. 8, Issue 12, pp. 75–82). https://doi.org/10.52403/ijrr.20211211

Data-Indian Trade Portal. (2020). Indian Trade Portal. https://www.indiantradeportal.in/%0Ahttp://www.indiantradeportal.in/index.jsp

Eni. (1967). In Angewandte Chemie International Edition, 6(11), 951–952. (Issue Mi, pp. 5–24). https://apeda.gov.in/apedawebsite/

Ministry of Commerce and Industry. (2014). Welcome to department of commerce, Government of India. In Ministry of Commerce and Industry. https://commerce.gov.in/about-us/divisions/export-products-division/export-products-agriculture/

Wicaksana, A., & Rachman, T. (2018). In Angewandte Chemie International Edition, 6(11), 951–952. (Vol. 3, Issue 1, pp. 10–27). https://medium.com/@arifwicaksanaa/pengertian-use-case-a7e576e1b6bf

Wicaksana, A., & Rachman, T. (2018). 済無No Title No Title No Title. In Angewandte Chemie International Edition, 6(11), 951–952. (Vol. 3, Issue 1, pp. 10–27). https://medium.com/@arifwicaksanaa/pengertian-use-case-a7e576e1b6bf

7

Government Initiatives to Boost Agricultural Exports

Pradeep Kumar Yadav and Nalin Kumar Mishra

Department of Agricultural Extension, TDPG College, Jaunpur Uttar Pradesh

Abstract

Government initiatives to boost agricultural exports are critical for driving economic growth, promoting rural development and enhancing food security. This paper provides an overview of the importance of such initiatives from various perspectives including economic growth, rural development, trade balance, food security, foreign investment, global competitiveness and environmental sustainability. It examines the strategic steps involved in government efforts, including policy formulation, market research, product development, infrastructure development, trade facilitation, export promotion, financial support, policy advocacy and monitoring and evaluation. Furthermore, the paper highlights common government initiatives implemented worldwide to enhance agricultural exports, such as trade agreements and negotiations, export promotion programs, market diversification efforts, quality and safety standards compliance, infrastructure development, financial support mechanisms, research and development investments, branding and certification promotion, sustainability and environmental stewardship and capacity building and training. Additionally, the advantages of government initiatives in boosting agricultural exports are discussed, including expanded market access, increased competitiveness, market diversification, better quality and safety standards, infrastructure development and financial support. However, the paper also acknowledges several limitations of these initiatives, including policy inconsistency, bureaucratic red tape, lack of coordination, limited access to finance, infrastructure deficiencies, market access barriers, environmental and social concerns and dependency on external factors.

Keywords: *Government Initiatives, Economic Growth, Rural Development, Trade Agreements, Export Promotion and Market Diversification*

Introduction

The agricultural sector of a country is significantly shaped by government activities, especially when it comes to exports. Globally, agricultural exports play a vital role in economic expansion, foreign exchange profits and rural development. The government has implemented a number of policies, initiatives and incentives to increase the export potential of agricultural products, acknowledging the significance of agricultural exports. These programs cover a broad spectrum of tactics, such as financial support mechanisms, trade agreements, market diversification measures, infrastructure development and regulatory reforms.

Recent years have seen rapid changes in the agricultural export scene brought about by shifting geopolitical conditions, technical breakthroughs and changing consumer needs. Global governments are paying more attention to making their nations more competitive in the realm of international agriculture trade. As a result, numerous programs have been launched with the goals of strengthening the position of farmers, increasing the effectiveness of the supply chain, raising the bar for product quality and safety and encouraging sustainability and innovation throughout the agricultural value chain.

This introduction looks at the wide range of government programs implemented in different nations to support agricultural exports. In order to maximize the export potential of their agricultural industries, reduce trade barriers, seize new market possibilities and solve issues with market access, competitiveness and sustainability, it looks at the many strategies that governments have taken.

In light of the growing global competitiveness and the need to feed an expanding population, governments are making greater use of their resources and knowledge to support agricultural exports as a catalyst for economic expansion and rural development. Stakeholders find opportunities for collaboration, innovation and market expansion in the agricultural sector by studying the methods and interventions used by governments to encourage agricultural exports. They can also get insights into the changing dynamics of international commerce.

Importance

Government initiatives to boost agricultural exports play a crucial role in driving economic growth, promoting rural development and enhancing food security. The importance of these initiatives can be understood from several perspectives:

1. **Economic Growth:** Agricultural exports support significantly to a country's overall economic growth by incresing foreign exchange earnings, creating employment opportunities along the value chain and stimulating investment in the agricultural sector. Government initiatives aimed at expanding export markets and increasing the competitiveness of agricultural products that can lead to higher export revenues, which in turn contribute to national income and GDP growth.
2. **Rural Development:** Agriculture is often the primary source of livelihood for rural communities, particularly in developing countries. Government initiatives to boost agricultural exports can benefit small farmers and rural households by providing access to lucrative export markets, improving farm incomes and reducing poverty. Moreover, investments in agricultural infrastructure, technology transfer and capacity building can enhance productivity and competitiveness in rural areas, thereby promoting inclusive and sustainable rural development.
3. **Trade Balance:** Agricultural exports play a crucial role in improving a country's trade balance by offsetting imports and generating surplus trade revenues. Government initiatives aimed at diversifying export markets, promoting value-added products and enhancing export competitiveness can help to reduce trade deficits and strengthen the overall balance of payments.
4. **Food Security:** Increased agricultural exports can contribute to food security by generating revenues that can be reinvested in domestic agricultural production, infrastructure and research. Moreover, export-oriented agriculture often focuses on high-value crops and value-added products, which can provide incentives for farmers to adopt modern farming practices, improve crop yields and enhance food production capacity.
5. **Foreign Investment:** A vibrant agricultural export sector can attract foreign investment in agribusiness, food processing and related industries, leading to technology transfer, job creation and economic diversification. Government initiatives that create an enabling environment for investment, such as export promotion schemes, trade agreements and investment incentives, can stimulate foreign direct investment (FDI) inflows and contribute to agricultural development and modernization.
6. **Global Competitiveness:** Government initiatives to boost agricultural exports can enhance a country's global competitiveness by promoting quality assurance, adherence to international standards and product

differentiation strategies. By facilitating market access, supporting branding and marketing efforts and providing export promotion services, governments can help agricultural exporters enter in international markets and compete effectively with global competitors

7. **Environmental Sustainability:** Sustainable agricultural exports require responsible stewardship of natural resources, conservation of biodiversity and adoption of eco-friendly farming practices. Government initiatives that promote sustainable agriculture, organic farming and environmental certification schemes can not only enhance the marketability of agricultural products but also contribute to environmental conservation and climate change mitigation efforts.

In summary, government initiatives to boost agricultural exports are essential for driving economic development, reducing poverty, enhancing food security and promoting sustainable agriculture. By providing policy support, financial incentives and institutional frameworks, governments can catalyze the growth of agricultural exports and unlock the sector's full potential as a driver of inclusive and sustainable development.

Fig: Steps involve in Agri-Exports by government

Strategic steps

Government initiatives to boost agricultural exports involve a series of strategic steps aimed at enhancing the competitiveness of agricultural products in global markets and facilitating trade. These steps typically include:

1. **Policy Formulation and Planning:** The government starts by formulating policies and developing strategic plans to promote agricultural exports. This involves assessing market opportunities, identifying target export markets, understanding trade barriers and formulating export promotion strategies. Policy frameworks may include trade agreements, tariff policies, export incentives and regulatory reforms aimed at facilitating exports.
2. **Market Research and Analysis:** Government agencies, in collaboration with industry stakeholders and trade associations, conduct market research and analysis to identify export opportunities and trends. This involves assessing demand-supply dynamics, consumer preferences, market access requirements

and competitive landscapes in target export markets. Market intelligence helps exporters make informed decisions and tailor their products to meet market demands.

3. **Product Development and Quality Assurance:** Governments support agricultural exporters in developing high-quality products that meet international standards and specifications. This may involve providing technical assistance, training programs and capacity-building initiatives to improve production practices, post-harvest handling, processing, packaging and quality control measures. Governments may also facilitate certification processes for organic, fair trade and other special products.
4. **Infrastructure Development:** Adequate infrastructure is essential for efficient and cost-effective agricultural exports. Governments invest in infrastructure development projects such as transportation networks (roads, railways, ports), cold chain facilities, storage warehouses and market infrastructure to support agricultural trade. Improving logistical efficiency reduces transportation costs, minimizes post-harvest losses and enhances the competitiveness of agricultural exports.
5. **Trade Facilitation:** Governments implement measures to streamline export procedures, reduce bureaucratic hurdles and facilitate trade transactions. This may include establishing one-stop export clearance centers, electronic documentation systems and online trade portals to simplify export processes and reduce administrative burdens on exporters. Trade facilitation measures aim to expedite customs clearance, reduce trade transaction costs and enhance the ease of doing business for exporters.
6. **Export Promotion and Marketing:** Governments undertake promotional activities to raise awareness of domestic agricultural products in international markets and facilitate market access. This may include organizing trade fairs, buyer-seller meets, promotional campaigns and participation in international exhibitions and trade missions. Governments also support exporters in branding, marketing and advertising initiatives to build their presence and reputation in target markets.
7. **Financial Support and Incentives:** Governments provide financial support and incentives to agricultural exporters to reduce risks, lower transaction costs and enhance competitiveness. This may include export credit facilities, export insurance schemes, export financing programs and export subsidy schemes aimed at offsetting export-related expenses,

such as transportation, marketing and quality certification costs.

8. **Policy Advocacy and Negotiations:** Governments advocate for the interests of agricultural exporters in international forums and negotiate trade agreements to secure favorable market access conditions. This involves engaging in bilateral and multilateral trade negotiations, addressing trade barriers, tariff reductions and non-tariff measures that impede agricultural exports. Governments also provide trade policy support, market access assistance and legal advice to exporters facing trade disputes or market access challenges.
9. **Monitoring and Evaluation:** Governments monitor the implementation and impact of export promotion initiatives through regular monitoring and evaluation mechanisms. This involves tracking export performance, assessing the effectiveness of export promotion programs and soliciting feedback from exporters and stakeholders. Monitoring and evaluation help governments identify areas for improvement, adjust policies and allocate resources more effectively to achieve export promotion objectives.

Government initiatives to boost agricultural exports

Government initiatives to boost agricultural exports vary widely depending on the specific needs, challenges and opportunities of each country's agricultural sector. Here are some common initiatives that governments around the world may implement to enhance agricultural exports:

1. **Trade Agreements and Negotiations:** Governments often engage in bilateral and multilateral trade agreements to reduce tariffs, quotas and other trade barriers that hinder agricultural exports. These agreements facilitate access to international markets and create a more favorable trading environment for agricultural producers.
2. **Export Promotion Programs:** Governments establish export promotion agencies or programs dedicated to supporting agricultural exporters. These programs provide financial assistance, market intelligence, trade missions and promotional activities to help farmers and agribusinesses penetrate new markets and expand their export reach.
3. **Market Diversification Efforts:** Governments encourage diversification of export markets to reduce reliance on a few key trading partners. This may involve identifying emerging markets, conducting market research and providing support to enter new markets through trade missions, promotional campaigns and matchmaking events.

4. **Quality and Safety Standards Compliance:** Governments implement measures to ensure that agricultural products meet the quality and safety standards of target export markets. This may involve providing technical assistance, capacity building and certification programs to help farmers comply with international standards and regulations.
5. **Infrastructure Development:** Governments invest in infrastructure projects to improve transportation, storage and handling facilities for agricultural products. This infrastructure development enhances supply chain efficiency, reduces post-harvest losses and lowers transaction costs, making agricultural exports more competitive in global markets.
6. **Financial Support Mechanisms:** Governments offer financial incentives such as export credits, insurance schemes and grants to support agricultural exporters. These financial support mechanisms help to reduce risks associated with exporting, provide working capital and encourage investment in export-oriented production and processing facilities.
7. **Research and Development Investments:** Governments allocate funding for research and development (R&D) initiatives aimed at enhancing the productivity, quality and competitiveness of agricultural products. R&D investments may focus on crop improvement, pest and disease management, value-added processing and sustainable agriculture practices to meet the evolving demands of export markets.
8. **Promotion of Branding and Certification:** Governments support initiatives to promote branding, certification and geographical indications (GI) for agricultural products with unique characteristics or origin. These branding efforts enhance the market value and competitiveness of agricultural products by highlighting their quality, authenticity and cultural heritage.
9. **Sustainability and Environmental Stewardship:** Governments promote sustainable agricultural practices and environmental stewardship to meet the growing demand for eco-friendly and ethically produced food products in export markets. This may involve providing incentives for organic farming, certification programs for sustainable agriculture and initiatives to reduce greenhouse gas emissions and environmental footprint.
10. **Capacity Building and Training:** Governments invest in capacity building and training programs to equip farmers, exporters and industry stakeholders with the knowledge, skills and resources needed to succeed in international markets. Training initiatives may cover topics such as

export regulations, market trends, value chain management and business development strategies.

Advantages of Government Initiatives to Boost Agricultural Exports:

1. **Expanded Market Access:** By lowering tariffs, quotas and other trade obstacles, government measures like trade agreements and talks can assist agricultural exporters in opening up new markets and increasing export potential.
2. **Increased Competitiveness:** By investing in R&D, infrastructure, quality control and marketing initiatives, government support programs and incentives can assist farmers in becoming more competitive.
3. **Market Diversification:** By reducing reliance on a small number of important trading partners, government initiatives to encourage market diversification can lessen the vulnerability of agricultural exports to disruptions in the market and local economic downturns.
4. **Better Quality and Safety Standards:** Government programs designed to guarantee adherence to global quality and safety standards can improve agricultural products' market acceptability and reputation, which can raise demand and prices in export markets.
5. **Infrastructure Development:** Agricultural exports can become more competitive in international markets by investing in infrastructure projects including processing, storage and transportation facilities. These investments can also decrease transaction costs, increase supply chain efficiency and minimize post-harvest losses.
6. **Financial Support**: Exporters of agricultural products can increase their export volumes, reduce the risks involved in exporting and overcome financial obstacles with the aid of government-funded export credits, insurance plans and grants.

Limitations of Government Initiatives to BoostAgricultural Exports:

1. **Policy Inconsistency:** Agricultural exporters may experience uncertainty as a result of changes to government policies and regulations pertaining to trade, taxes, subsidies and export incentives, which may jeopardize long-term planning and investment decisions.
2. **Bureaucratic Red Tape:** The competitiveness of exporters can be adversely affected by excessive bureaucracy and administrative obstacles in acquiring permits, licenses and certifications, which can impede agricultural exports, raise transaction costs and cause shipments to be delayed.

3. **Lack of Coordination:** The efficacy of export activities may be limited by fragmented or poorly coordinated government departments in charge of trade promotion, export facilitation and agricultural development. These agencies may have overlapping missions, inefficiencies and duplication of efforts.
4. **Limited Access to Finance:** Due to strict lending requirements and a lack of credit availability, agricultural exporters—especially small and medium-sized firms (SMEs)—may still have difficulty obtaining inexpensive finance for export-related operations even with the financial support mechanisms offered by governments.
5. **Infrastructure Deficiencies:** The capacity and efficiency of agricultural supply chains can be limited by a lack of investment in infrastructure development, which includes transportation, storage and cold chain facilities. This can result in bottlenecks, delays and quality losses in export operations.
6. **Market Access Barriers:** For agricultural exporters, sanitary and phytosanitary (SPS) measures, non-tariff barriers and technical requirements imposed by importing nations can present serious difficulties. These measures can limit market access for certain products and need expensive compliance efforts.
7. **Environmental and Social Concerns:** Sometimes, government programs to increase agricultural exports put short-term financial gain ahead of long-term sustainability and environmental stewardship, which has a detrimental effect on local communities, biodiversity and natural resources.
8. **Dependency on External Factors:** The effectiveness of government programs aimed at increasing agricultural exports may be impacted by outside variables that are out of policymakers' control, such as changes in the world market, fluctuations in currency rates, geopolitical unrest and natural disasters.

Conclusion

In conclusion, government initiatives aimed at bolstering agricultural exports are essential drivers of economic growth, rural development and food security globally. These initiatives encompass a wide array of strategies, ranging from policy formulation to infrastructure development and export promotion programs. The significance of these efforts is underscored by their multifaceted impact on various aspects of society, including job creation, poverty reduction and trade balance improvement. By investing in infrastructure such as transportation networks and storage facilities, governments enhance the efficiency and competitiveness of agricultural supply chains, reducing post-harvest losses and transaction costs. Moreover, measures to ensure compliance with quality and safety standards enable agricultural products to meet the stringent requirements of international markets, thereby enhancing market access and competitiveness. Market diversification efforts further mitigate risks associated with over-reliance on a limited number of trading partners, fostering resilience in the face of economic uncertainties. Despite their undeniable advantages, government initiatives face challenges such as policy inconsistency and bureaucratic hurdles, necessitating continuous efforts to streamline processes and improve coordination among stakeholders. Nevertheless, the potential of these initiatives to drive inclusive and sustainable development remains immense, particularly in the context of evolving global challenges such as climate change and geopolitical shifts. Through sustained commitment to innovation, collaboration and sustainability, governments can harness the full potential of agricultural exports to address pressing societal needs and foster a more prosperous and resilient future for all.

References

Alston, J. M., & Martin, P. L. (2018). Trade and agricultural competitiveness: A view from the United States. American Journal of Agricultural Economics, 100(5), 1293-1313.

Anderson, K., & Nelgen, S. (2019). Global trade and food safety: Winners and losers in a fragmented system. Food Policy, 84, 52-62.

Babcock, B. A. (2018). The impacts of agricultural trade on food security. Annual Review of Resource Economics, 10, 217-235.

Bureau, J. C., & Swinnen, J. (2019). Global agricultural trade and developing countries. World Development, 120, 1-1.

Cadot, O., & Malouche, M. (2018). Trade policies, household welfare and poverty alleviation: A general equilibrium analysis applied to the case of Egypt. World Development, 108, 243-259.

Food and Agriculture Organization of the United Nations (FAO). "The future of food and agriculture – Alternative pathways to 2050," The Future of Food and Agriculture 319842, Food and Agriculture Organization of the United Nations, Agricultural Development Economics Division (ESA).

Fuglie, K., & Wang, S. L. (2019). Productivity growth in global agriculture slowing down. American Journal of Agricultural Economics, 101(2), 514-533.

Maertens, M., & Swinnen, J. (Eds.). (2019). Globalization, poverty and inequality: Between a rock and a hard place. Oxford University Press.

Nicholas E. Rada & Steven T. Buccola & Keith O. Fuglie, 2010. "Government Policy and Agricultural Productivity in Indonesia," American Journal of Agricultural Economics, Agricultural and Applied Economics Association, vol. 93(3), pages 863-880.

8

Trade's Hidden Hurdles: Unraveling the Complexities of SPS and TBT Measures

Harishankar. K

Agricultural Economics, Department of Social Science, Vanavarayar Institute of Agriculture, Pollachi, Tamil Nadu

Abstract

Non-tariff barrier (NTBs), particularly Sanitary and Phytosanitary (SPS) measures and Technical Barriers to Trade (TBT), have increasingly shaped the contours of international trade. While originally instituted to safeguard human, animal, and plant health and ensure product standards, these regulatory mechanisms are often criticized for functioning as covert instruments of protectionism. This chapter undertakes a comprehensive analysis of the dual nature of SPS and TBT measures, acknowledging their public policy rationale while critically examining their role in distorting trade flows, increasing compliance burdens, and eroding competitiveness, especially for exporters in developing economies. It highlights the economic ramifications, operational challenges, and policy complexities inherent in their implementation. Drawing from global best practices and multilateral frameworks, the study advocates for targeted strategies such as regulatory harmonization, improved transparency, enhanced capacity-building and robust dispute resolution mechanisms. These approaches are essential not only to prevent the misuse of SPS and TBT provisions but also to facilitate equitable market access and support a rules based international trading system. The chapter emphasizes that achieving this balance is critical for fostering inclusive economic growth, promoting global competitiveness, and strengthening cooperation among nations in an increasingly interconnected world.

Keywords: *Non-Tariff Barriers (NTBs), Sanitary and Photosanitary Measures (SPS), Technical Barriers to Trade (TBT), Regulatory Harmonization and Disguised Protectionism*

1. Introduction

In the contemporary interconnected global economy, international trade serves as a pivotal driver of economic growth and prosperity across nations (Coe and

Yeung, 2015). As globalization burgeons, trade negotiations and agreements have predominantly centered on the reduction of traditional trade barriers, notably tariffs (Bagwell and Staiger, 2013). However, non-tariff barriers (NTBs) have emerged as formidable challenges that have the potential to obstruct the movement of goods, services, and investments across international borders. Among these NTBs, two categories - sanitary and phytosanitary (SPS) measures and technical barriers to trade (TBT) - have assumed increasing prominence due to their capacity to disrupt the dynamics of global trade (Kang and Ramizo, 2017).

SPS measures primarily aim to protect the health and safety of humans, animals, and plants, encompassing regulations pertaining to food safety, animal health, plant health, and disease control (Khetarpal, 2016). On the other hand, TBT measures encompass a range of product standards and technical regulations that products must adhere to for market eligibility. While both SPS and TBT measures are founded on essential public policy objectives, they may inadvertently be manipulated as protectionist instruments, thereby posing significant challenges to international trade (Ruckteschler, 2022).

This research article embarks on a comprehensive exploration of the intricate landscape of SPS and TBT measures. It scrutinizes their influence on the global trade milieu, unravels the underlying complexities and challenges tied to their implementation, and prescribes a compendium of strategic initiatives to mitigate these non-tariff barriers. Striking a balance that allows nations to uphold public welfare while fostering international trade for the collective benefit of the global community is of paramount importance.

The Impact of SPS and TBT Measures on Global Trade

Economic Implications

SPS and TBT measures wield substantial economic clout, impacting not only businesses but also consumers and governments. These measures introduce an element of unpredictability and intricacy into international trade, engendering a spectrum of economic ramifications:

Increased Compliance Costs: Exporters are mandated to adhere to an array of standards and regulations to access foreign markets. Navigating these diverse and often stringent requirements incurs elevated compliance costs, which are particularly onerous for small and medium-sized enterprises (SMEs). These costs encompass expenditures associated with testing, certification, and compliance documentation (Seyoum, 2017).

Export Delays: SPS and TBT measures can engender delays at border crossings as products undergo scrutiny and validation. These delays disrupt supply chains, augment inventory holding costs, and diminish the reliability of just-in-time production systems (Kogan, 2005).

Eroded Competitiveness: The cumulative effect of compliance costs and delays can erode the competitiveness of businesses in international markets. Inefficiencies within trade procedures can pose challenges for companies aiming to compete on a global scale (Leonidou, 2004).

Consumer Price Effects: Ultimately, the expenses borne by businesses to surmount SPS and TBT measures are frequently passed on to consumers in the form of higher prices for imported goods. This phenomenon can contribute to an augmented cost of living for consumers (Deodhar, 2001).

Disguised Protectionism

One of the most pressing concerns associated with SPS and TBT measures is their susceptibility to manipulation as tools of concealed protectionism. Nations may impose ostensibly stringent standards and certification procedures not solely to protect public health and safety, but also to insulate domestic industries from foreign competition (Hufbauer, 2013). This manifestation of protectionism can unleash several detrimental effects:

Market Access Constraints: Rigorous and potentially unwarranted standards can pose significant barriers to entry for foreign products, constraining their market access (Hoekman, and Mavroidis, 1996). This restriction can distort trade patterns and inflict harm upon exporters from other countries.

Trade Distortions: Concealed protectionism can distort the dynamics of global trade, precipitating suboptimal resource allocation. Inefficient domestic industries may be shielded from international competition, thereby curbing incentives for innovation and the enhancement of productivity (Mariotti, 2022).

Impediments to Economic Growth: By constricting competition and innovation, concealed protectionism can impede economic growth within both the protectionist nation and its trade partners.

Challenges Surrounding SPS and TBT Measures

Lack of Harmonization

An inherent challenge in addressing SPS and TBT measures lies in the absence of harmonization among nations. Divergent regulations, standards, and certification procedures coalesce to engender substantial trade barriers and compliance quandaries for exporters (Cadot *et al.,* 2012). Although international organizations like the World Trade Organization (WTO) have established frameworks to tackle these issues, attaining harmonization proves to be a formidable endeavor due to:

Diverse Regulatory Goals: Nations may harbor distinct public health and safety objectives, culminating in divergent standards and regulations.

Technical Hurdles: The attainment of harmonization necessitates an intricate comprehension of the technical and scientific dimensions intertwined with health and safety, rendering it a daunting challenge.

Political Considerations: The sphere of harmonization can be influenced by political considerations, rendering consensus on shared standards a complex task.

Resource Deficiencies: Developing nations, in particular, may grapple with resource and technical expertise constraints, rendering alignment of their regulations with international standards a herculean undertaking (Head, 2022).

Transparency and Information Sharing

Transparency and information sharing constitute pivotal components in tackling SPS and TBT issues. Several nations encounter a paucity of transparency in their regulatory processes, constructing an environment wherein exporters wrestle with anticipation and compliance. Notable challenges in this arena encompass:

Opaque Decision-Making: In select instances, the decision-making processes underpinning the imposition of SPS and TBT measures lack transparency, rendering it intricate for affected parties to discern the rationale and necessity of these measures.

Notification Gaps: Certain nations inadequately notify trading partners of proposed SPS and TBT measures in a timely manner, thereby engendering last-minute compliance predicaments for exporters.

Data Accessibility: The availability and accessibility of data and scientific information underpinning these measures can exhibit substantial variations, further complicating transparency endeavors (Stone and Casalini, 2020 & Prinja *et al.,* 2018).

Capacity Building

Developing nations frequently confront significant capacity constraints concerning the implementation and compliance with SPS and TBT measures. These constraints manifest on multifarious fronts:

Technical Expertise: A myriad of developing nations lacks the technical prowess requisite for the effective evaluation and implementation of intricate SPS and TBT measures.

Infrastructural Shortcomings: Inadequate infrastructure, paucity of laboratories, and testing facilities can impede compliance with standards and regulations.

Human Capital Deficits: An inadequacy of skilled personnel in domains such as food safety, animal health, and plant health can impede capacity building efforts.

Resource Impediments: Developing nations may grapple with the allocation of financial and human resources requisite for enhancing their capacity to comply with SPS and TBT measures (Fukuda-Parr and Lopes, 2013).

Strategies to Address SPS and TBT Issues

International Cooperation and Standardization

The redressal of SPS and TBT issues demands a foundation of international cooperation and standardization. Vital strategies in this context encompass:

Augmented Multilateral Engagement: Nations should reaffirm their commitment to multilateral accords such as the WTO's Agreement on the Application of Sanitary and Phytosanitary Measures (SPS Agreement) and the Agreement on Technical Barriers to Trade (TBT Agreement), fostering cooperation and harmonization (Kohl *et al.,* 2016).

Adoption of International Standards: Encouraging nations to align their domestic regulations with established international standards, including those formulated by the Codex Alimentarius Commission and pertinent international standards bodies, can foster augmented harmonization (Pekdemir, 2018).

Peer Review Mechanisms: The establishment of peer review mechanisms permitting nations to assess the compliance of their counterparts with international standards can promote transparency and the adoption of best practices (Paulo and Reisen, 2010).

4.2. Transparency Mechanisms

Enhancing transparency mechanisms emerges as a sine qua non for ameliorating the predictability of SPS and TBT measures. Pertinent strategies comprise:

Online Databases: Nations should maintain up-to-date online databases housing information regarding SPS and TBT measures, encompassing draft regulations, for facile access by stakeholders, including businesses and other governments (Pauwelyn *et al.,* 2016).

Notification Systems: The development of robust notification systems mandating timely and comprehensive notifications to trading partners regarding proposed SPS and TBT measures can amplify transparency (Wolfe, 2020).

Consultation Procedures: The institution of consultation procedures enabling stakeholders to contribute input on proposed measures can ensure the reasonableness of regulations, anchoring them in scientific foundations while accommodating the interests of all stakeholders.

Capacity Building and Technical Assistance

Capacity building and technical assistance initiatives warrant prioritization to empower developing nations to meet international standards. Vital strategies encompass:

Training Programs: Conception and implementation of training programs intensifying the technical expertise of individuals involved in the implementation of SPS and TBT measures prove invaluable.

Infrastructure Augmentation: Investment in laboratory facilities, the bolstering of testing infrastructure, and the augmentation of inspection capabilities can aid developing nations in meeting the requirements of international standards.

Knowledge Transfer: The facilitation of knowledge transfer through partnerships and collaborations between developed and developing nations can accelerate capacity building endeavors.

Resource Mobilization: Support rendered to developing nations in resource mobilization for SPS and TBT compliance constitutes an essential facet of their seamless integration into the global trading landscape (Braganza *et al.,* 2009).

4.4. Dispute Resolution Mechanisms

Efficient dispute resolution mechanisms furnish a quintessential apparatus for addressing instances of non-compliance or the misuse of SPS and TBT measures. Salient strategies encompass:

Strengthened WTO Dispute Settlement: The reinforcement and streamlining of dispute settlement procedures within the WTO can ensure the fair and expeditious resolution of disputes related to SPS and TBT measures (Mavroidis, 2022).

Alternative Dispute Resolution: Exploration of alternative dispute resolution mechanisms, including mediation and arbitration, can proffer more flexible and expeditious resolutions to disputes intertwined with SPS and TBT (Mercurio, 2004).

Conclusion

In summation, non-tariff barriers, prominently featuring SPS and TBT measures, have materialized as pivotal challenges in international trade. While safeguarding human, animal, and plant health stands as a legitimate and imperative objective, it is equally vital to strike an equilibrium that permits the seamless flow of goods and services across international borders. Addressing SPS and TBT issues necessitates concerted endeavors at both the national and international echelons. To efficaciously dismantle these non-tariff barriers, the global community must prioritize harmonization, transparency, and capacity enhancement. By endorsing these principles and fostering international collaboration, nations can ensure the legitimate utilization of SPS and TBT measures while facilitating international trade, thereby serving the mutual benefit of all stakeholders. However, it is incumbent upon us to acknowledge that the path forward shall not be bereft of challenges. Varying national interests, the intricacies of technology, and resource constraints shall continue to present formidable impediments. Nonetheless, the exigency of addressing SPS and TBT issues is unmistakable, especially in the backdrop of an increasingly intertwined global economy. Through collaborative endeavors, nations can chart a course towards a more open and equitable global trading milieu, thereby catalyzing economic growth and enhancing the well-being of both developed and developing nations.

References

Bagwell, K., & Staiger, R. W. (2013). Can the Doha round be a development round? Setting a place at the table. In Globalization in an age of crisis: Multilateral economic cooperation in the twenty-first century (pp. 91-124). University of Chicago Press.

Cadot, O., Malouche, M., & Sáez, S. (2012). Streamlining non-tariff measures: a toolkit for policy makers. World Bank Publications.

Coe, N. M., & Yeung, H. W. C. (2015). Global production networks: Theorizing economic development in an interconnected world. Oxford University Press.

Head, B. W. (2022). Wicked problems in public policy. Springer International Publishing.

Kohl, T., Brakman, S., & Garretsen, H. (2016). Do trade agreements stimulate international trade differently? Evidence from 296 trade agreements. The World Economy, 39(1), 97-131.

Braganza, A., Hackney, R., & Tanudjojo, S. (2009). Organizational knowledge transfer through creation, mobilization and diffusion: a case analysis of InTouch within Schlumberger. Information Systems Journal, 19(5), 499-522.

Deodhar, S. Y. (2001). WTO Agreements on SPS and TBT: Implications for Food Quality Issues.

Fukuda-Parr, S., & Lopes, C. (Eds.). (2013). Capacity for development: new solutions to old problems. Routledge.

Hoekman, B. M., & Mavroidis, P. C. (1996). Dumping, antidumping and antitrust. J. World Trade, 30, 27.

Hufbauer, G. C., Schott, J. J., & Cimino-Isaacs, C. (2013). Local content requirements: A global problem (Vol. 102). Columbia University Press.

Kang, J. W., & Ramizo, D. M. (2017). Impact of sanitary and phytosanitary measures and technical barriers on international trade. Journal of World Trade, 51(4).

Khetarpal, R. (2016). Converging Provisions of CBD and WTO to Ensure Agricultural Biosecurity. Indian Journal of Plant Genetic Resources, 29(3), 407-409.

Kogan, L. A. (2005). How Europe employs disguised regulatory protectionism to weaken American free enterprise. International Journal of Economic Development, 7(2-3), 65-412.

Leonidou, L. C. (2004). An analysis of the barriers hindering small business export development. Journal of small business management, 42(3), 279-302.

Mariotti, S. (2022). A warning from the Russian–Ukrainian war: avoiding a future that rhymes with the past. Journal of Industrial and Business Economics, 49(4), 761-782.

Mavroidis, P. C. (2022). The WTO dispute settlement system: how, why and where?. Edward Elgar Publishing.

Mercurio, B. (2004). Improving dispute settlement in the World Trade Organization: the dispute settlement understanding review-making it work. J. World Trade, 38, 795.

Paulo, S., & Reisen, H. (2010). Eastern donors and western soft law: Towards a DAC donor peer review of China and India?. Development Policy Review, 28(5), 535-552.

Pauwelyn, J. H., Guzman, A., & Hillman, J. A. (2016). International trade law. Aspen Publishing.

Pekdemir, C. (2018). On the regulatory potential of regional organic standards: Towards harmonization, equivalence, and trade?. Global environmental change, 50, 289-302.

Prinja, S., Downey, L. E., Gauba, V. K., & Swaminathan, S. (2018). Health technology assessment for policy making in India: current scenario and way forward. PharmacoEconomics-Open, 2, 1-3.

Ruckteschler, C., Malik, A., & Eibl, F. (2022). Politics of trade protection in an autocracy: Evidence from an EU tariff liberalization in Morocco. European Journal of Political Economy, 71, 102063.

Seyoum, B. (2017). Export controls and international business: a study with special emphasis on dual-use export controls and their impact on firms in the US. Journal of Economic Issues, 51(1), 45-72.

Stone, S., & Casalini, F. (2020). Sanitary and phytosanitary measures. Handbook of Deep Trade Agreements, 367.

Wolfe, R. (2020). Reforming WTO conflict management: Why and how to improve the use of 'specific trade concerns'. Journal of International Economic Law, 23(4), 817-839.

9

Empowering FPO'S for Agricultural Export Success: Key Strategic Imperatives

[1]Prabhavathi, Y., [2]Krishna Kishore, N.T, [3]K Nirmal Ravi Kumar [4]Rajesh, A

[1]Department of Agribusiness Management, Advanced Post Graduate Centre Acharya N G Ranga Agricultural University, Guntur, Andhra Pradesh
[2]Agri Finance and R & D Specialist, UNDP, India
[3]Department of Agricultural Economics, S V Agricultural College ANGRAU, Tirupati, Andhra Pradesh
[4]Department of Agricultural Entomology, S V Agricultural College ANGRAU, Tirupati, Andhra Pradesh

Abstract

The agricultural sector in India is predominantly characterized by small and marginal landholders who face numerous challenges, including limited access to markets, resources, and technology. Farmer Producer Organizations (FPOs) have emerged as a collective model to address these challenges, enabling farmers to achieve economies of scale and enhance market linkages. This study explores the strategic imperatives for empowering FPO's to access international markets, focusing on their ability to improve business capacities, adopt global standards, and invest in infrastructure. Key strategies include nurturing FPOs through competency development, resource pooling, and collaborations with institutions and private players. The paper highlights the importance of integrating FPOs into global value chains, enhancing their market adaptability, and fostering long-term sustainability through community-driven investments. The findings underscore that tailored support and strategic interventions can transform FPOs into viable entities capable of driving economic growth and improving the well-being of small-scale farmers.

Keywords: *Farmer Producer Organizations (FPOs), Agricultural Value Chains, International Market Access, Resource Pooling and Market Adaptability*

Introduction

Small and marginal land holders account for86.08 per cent of total operational holdings in India. The land holdings of these small holders shrunksignificantly from 2.28 hectares in 1970-71 to just 1.08 hectares in 2015-16, reflecting a growing fragmentation of land ownership(GoI, 2020). These fragmented small holders are confronted with multiple challenges both on input and output markets. They are face challengessuch as limited access to quality inputs, markets, credit, information, extension services, technical knowhow besides lacking in bargaining power, technology adoption, capital investment and value addition activities. These challenges have hindered their ability to leverage economies of scale, thereby limiting their share in the consumer rupee due to elevated transaction costs. (Singh & Singh, 2013; Loeper et al., 2016). However, earlier reports suggested that collectivization of these small holders into various collective organizations such as cooperatives, farmers clubs, producer organizations (POs) serves as an efficient mechanism in addressing the challenges of these resource scarce farmers while improving their incomes and wellbeing (Trebbin & Hassler2012; Vadivelu & Kiran, 2013). But, the viability of these collectives is uncertain without external assistance and continuous support, as their members not only lack resources but also possess limited bargaining power and a limited understanding of market dynamics. Furthermore, extended marketing support to these collectives result in greater improvement in income levels compared to production-orientedsupport. Further if these types of collective organizations if properly nurtured, mentored and supported they not only access the domestic markets but also gain the potential to tap export markets as they move forward in their value chain. Among various forms of farmer collectives, farmer producer organizations (FPOs) hold greater potential for tapping into the export market due to their intrinsic structure and external policy support.

Farmer Producer Organizations

Among various collectivization forms, Producer Organization (PO) is one such organization formed by primary producers who are farmers (agriculture, horticulture, dairy, animal husbandry, apiary, fisheries etc) and produce either farm or non-farm based. If the members of the producer organization are farmers, then the PO is called as farmer producer organization (FPO) (NABARD, 2015). In response to poor performance of traditional agricultural cooperatives, a high-level committee led by Y. K. Alagha recommended for conversion of cooperative businesses into companies through incorporation of cooperatives as companies while still preserving the distincr elements of cooperative business. Accordingly, Govt of India amendment the Companies Act of 1956, i.e Companies (Amendment) Act, 2002 by inserting an additional part "Part IX A" leading to incorporation of 'Producer Company'. Those FPOs that get registered under Companies act are farmer producer companies (FPCs).However, in India, Farmer Producer Organizations (FPOs) have the flexibility to choose registration under various legal frameworks, including the Cooperative Society Act, Companies Act, Society Act, or Indian Trust Act. But FPOs registered under the Companies Act or Cooperative Society Act are legally allowed to distribute profits among their members, whereas those registered under other frameworks are typically considered non-profit entities.

Table 1: Total number of FPOs in India (as on 31.03.2022)

Sl.No.	Agencies promoting FPO's	Total No.
1	SFAC	892
2	NABARD	3904
3	SFAC, NABARD, NCDC under central sector scheme	2257
4	NRLM Programme	182
5	Other Implementing agencies (State Governments/ Other Organizations/Trust/Foundations)	2069
	Total	**9034**

Source: Authors compilation from secondary data sources

Business Activities of FPO's in India

FPOs either by themselves or in facilitation from promoting agencies establish forward and backward linkages in the agri value chain. These FPOs through establishing such linkages perform various roles in the agricultural value chain majorly to address the production and marketing constraints of small holders. The type of business operations performed by FPOs depends on the capabilities and competencies of managerial team, experiences of promoting organizations, magnitude of the problem identified in the operational area, resource pooling capacity of members, readiness for application of pooled resources and so on. The business operations identified by FPOs decide their efficiency and role in agriculture value chain to impact the member farmers

In India, the business activities of FPOs are majorly of selling farm inputs while also playing the aggregator role either for better bargaining or supplying directly to government agencies without any middlemen to certain extent (Prasad, 2019; Singh, 2021b). Majority of FPOs engaged in upstream value chain activities primarily rely on ensuring timely supply of agricultural inputs at slightly lower prices than their competitors through establishing backward linkages. Few FPOs in this stream are also undertaking businesses of seed production and manufacturing of bio related inputs to a minimal extent.

Further, they are also acting as facilitators inproviding range of services that include technical know-how, crop advisory, financial, custom hiring and other capacity building to support farmers. Their primary focus remains on production-centric businesses and services, with their target market primarily comprising internal farmer members themselves.

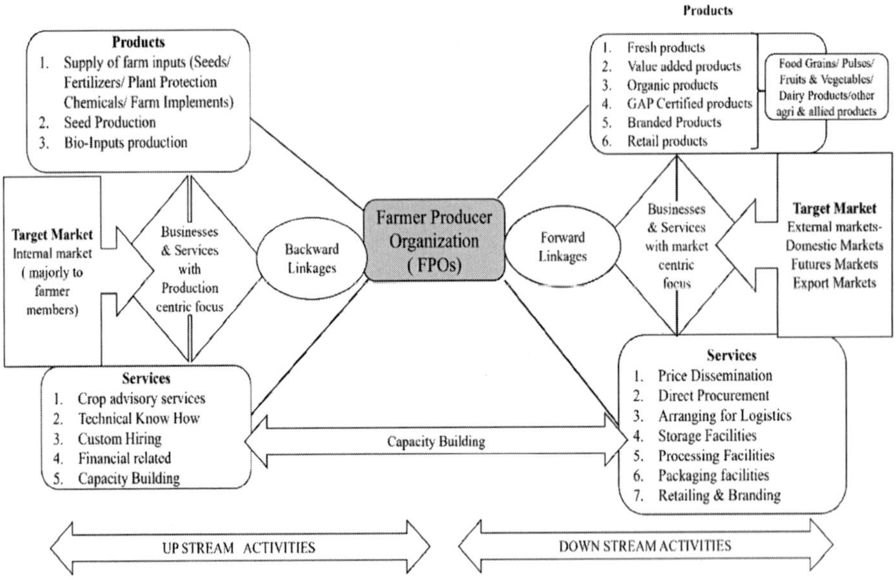

Fig. 1: Business activities of FPOs in agri value chain

A significant portion of Farmer Producer Organizations (FPOs) engaged in downstream value chain activities primarily focus on marketing a diverse range of agricultural productsby establishing forward linkages These products encompass fresh produce, value-added goods, organic items, GAP-certified products, branded and retail offerings of food grains, pulses, fruits, vegetables, dairy products, and various other agricultural and allied products. Further, these FPOs offer facilitation services such as price dissemination, and engaging in direct farm procurement to supply products directly to government procurement agencies, agricultural startups, traders, and corporate entities, among others.Some FPOs in this category are progressing along their value chain by engaging in need-based primary processing operations like grading, sorting, and logistics, as well as secondary and tertiary processing activities related to value addition, packaging, branding, and retailing.Their primary focus remains on market-centric businesses and services, with their target market primarily comprising domestic, futures and export markets. Those

FPOs whose business operations are more of market centric are able to link themselves to alternate markets resulting in better higher economic benefits through effectively reducing the output transaction costs, enhanced bargaining power and better price realization. (Fischer & Qaim, 2012; Prathiban et al., 2015; Latynskiy & Berger, 2016; Pingali et al., 2019)

Advantages of FPO's in accessing international markets

Farmer Producer Organizations (FPOs) play a vital role in enhancing the ability of resource poor small and marginal farmers to access the international markets. The advantages to FPOs in accessing export markets include:

i. **Understanding Export Dynamics**: Business Engagingin export markets enhances the business capacities of FPOsenabling them to gain a better understanding of the evolving dynamics of export markets, including quality standards, consumer preferences, and market trends.

ii. **Compliance and Regulation**:Involvement in export markets necessitates FPOs in understanding the significance of adhering regulatory and statutory requirements both in domestic and export markets. This fosters a deeper understanding of international trade regulations, documentation, and compliance obligations.

iii. **Quality Control and Sustainability**: Participation in export markets ensures FPOs to implement quality control measures such as good agricultural practices (GAP) and other sustainable farming practices to ensure that the output meeting the standardsthereby enabling them to fetch higher prices.

iv. **Institutional and Financial Linkages**: Access to international markets enables FPOs to establish stronger institutional and financial linkages for better understanding of markets, potential buyers and as well aware of financial and non-financial supportincluding incentives, subsidies and export credit facilities.

v. **Investing in infrastructure**: Participation in export markets encourages FPOs to strongly invest in infrastructure facilities like cold storage, warehouses, primary processing, transportationto address the inherent challenges of perishability, standardization, grading, quality control.

vi. **Technology and Traceability**: Participation in export markets encourages FPOs to collaborate with national and international players to enhance traceability in the food supply chains for high value products. This necessitates investment in technologies such as IoT, block chain etc.

vii. **Negotiation and Networking**: Access to international markets allows FPOs to establish networking with export channels such as exporters and importers for better price negotiation and higher price realization.

viii. **Diversification**: Accessing international markets empowers FPOs to diversify their business by bringing multiple commodities into their portfolio and expand business in long run

ix. **Brand Building**: Participation in export markets helps FPOs to focus on brand buildingactivities to gain trust and recognition in the international markets

x. **Market Adoptability**: Accessing international markets helps FPOs to be more dynamic in understanding the market dynamics, market risks and tailor their activities accordingly.

xi. **Economies of Scale**: Accessing international markets helps FPOs to gain economies of scale through pooling more producc and exporting in larger quantities to meet the demands of international markets

xii. **Global Best Practices**: Accessing international markets helps FPOs to get exposed to global business practices that include certifications, quality standards, packaging requirements, etc.

xiii. **Asset Utilization Efficiency**: Accessing international markets enables the scope of asset utilization efficiency through maximizing infrastructure utilization year-round

xiv. **Capital Formation**: Accessing international markets facilitates capital formation directly at production centers, which werepreviously situated closer to market hubs.

xv. **Domestic market Enhancement**: Accessing international markets fosters improvement in domestic markets as a result of the spillover effects resulting from the adoption of global standards in areas such as packaging, quality, and certification.

xvi. **Value Creation**: Participation in international markets fostersvalue creation through certification particularly in terms of geographical indicators, traceability of food products and others

Nurturing FPOs to Participate in Global Markets

Several researches on FPO reported that in addition to capital, FPOs are lacking in business skills and capacities for effectively undertaking upstream and downstream business operations and create value for farmers (Mahajan, 2015). Furthermore, FPOs are operating with poor governance while lacking professionalism in their management, have poor sense of ownership, business acumen and operating with unsuitable business models (Govil et al., 2020; NABARD, 2022; Shree & Vaishnavi, 2022; Singh, 2022). FPO promoting organizations namely cluster-based business organizations (CBBOs) are majorly undertaking activities related to member mobilization, meeting legal and regulatory compliances and undertaking those businesses that has provisions of grants and subsidies. Hence, FPOs and their promoting organizations has to be nurtured well with commercial business orientation emphasizingself-reliance and sustained growth and as well addressing the challenges essential for accessing export markets. Ways to nurture FPOsencompass:

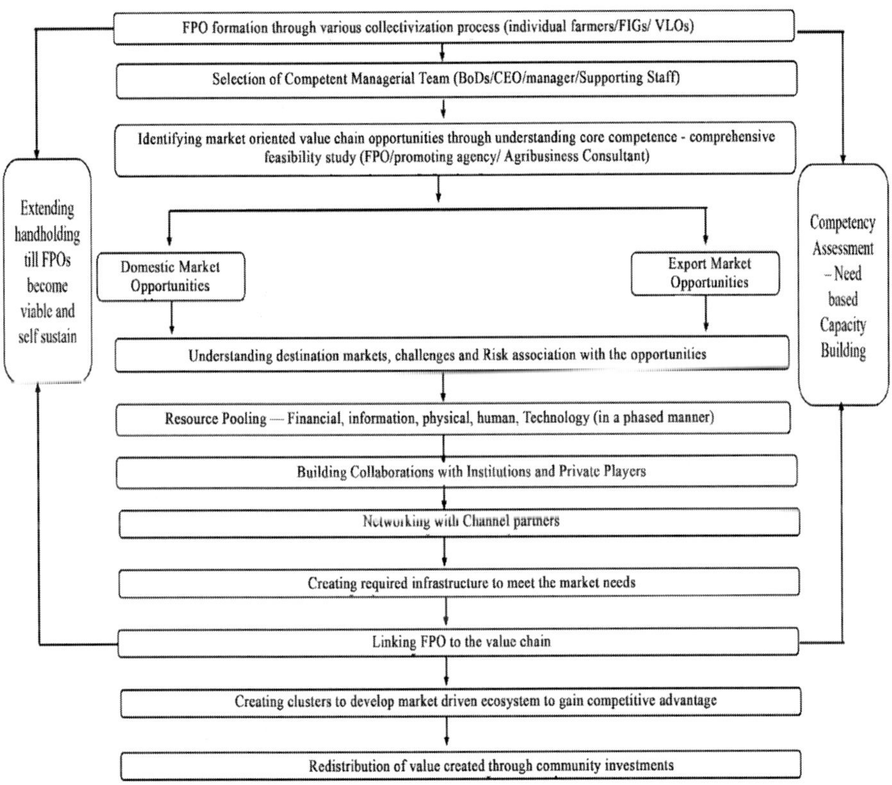

Fig. 2: Strategic Imperatives in Nurturing FPOs to access global markets

i. **FPO formation through various collectivization process:** Thecollectivization process of farmers to form into FPOs is generally of three forms. Farmers either by themselves get mobilized and form into FPO. In the second form, the promoting agencies form farmers into small informal groups of 15 to 20 members called as farmer interest groups (FIGs) and these FIGs get mobilized to form as FPO. In the third scenario, promoting agencies mobilize pre-existing large village-level informal groups, comprising 100 to 200 members, known as Village Level Organizations (VLOs), to come together and establish FPOs (Prabhavathi et al., 2022)

ii. **Selection of Competent Managerial Team:** FPOs need to select a competent managerial team for effectively managing the internal and external business operations. While selecting members for managerial roles (board of directors, CEO/managers and other supporting staff),priority should be placed on factors such as education, prior business experience, leadership roles within community-based organizations, and a demonstrated interest in social media platforms. These criteria should take precedence over considerations like age, farm size, and exposure to mass media. (Prabhavathi, 2023)

iii. **Identifying market-oriented value chain opportunities through understanding core competence - comprehensive feasibility study:** The core competencies of any organization, including farm businesses, play a crucial role in gaining a competitive edge in the market, and this is particularly significant when entering international markets. The core competencies of farm business are majorly derived from nature of commodity produced which inturn depends on climatic conditions, geographic locations, farming practices (organic or natural) evolved overtime,commercial orientation of local farmers (Chilli, Cotton, Turmeric farmers in Andhra Pradesh), geographical indicators (Araku Coffee, Palasa Cashew), certifications etc… FPOs before undertaking business operations need to conduct a detailed feasibility study aimed at identifying the value chain opportunities through understanding the core competencies. Engaging the services of agribusiness consultants can enhance the effectiveness the feasibility study and the overall strategic planning process. Understanding of these factors enables FPOs to identify the market opportunities domestically and globally, allowing them to strategically prioritize their efforts, directing their focus toward either domestic or export markets.

iv. **Understanding destination markets, challenges and risks associated with the opportunities**: Once FPOs prioritize their focus, it is crucial for them to have a deep understanding of destination markets, challenges and risks associated with the opportunities.Particularly, FPOs venturing into export markets must attain a clear understanding of these markets in terms of their scale, growth prospects, competition landscape, market demands,prevailing consumer preferences, and comparative core competence with similar markets. Simultaneously, they must remain vigilant regarding potential risks, encompassing legal, political, regulatory, and statutory requisites, as well as phytosanitary standards and trade agreements that may impact their export endeavors.Further, the threats associated in the area also need to be assessed accordingly. Collaborating with expert organizations and agribusiness consultants can greatly facilitate this multifaceted process.

v. **Resource Pooling:** Unlike all business organizations, FPOs also face resource scarcity. But this should not pull back in leveraging their opportunities. Resources, ranging from financial and informational to physical, human, and technological, play a pivotal role in harnessing identified opportunities.Among various resources, information plays a key role particularly in understanding export markets. FPOs should adopt a strategic approach to resource pooling, encompassing both financial and non-financial aspects, with a well-defined action plan for each phase of their operations

   Pooling of human resources to enables FPOs to effectively undertake business operations while pooling of physical and technological infrastructure enables to optimize their production and post production processes while minimizing transaction costs. Nevertheless, for resource pooling to be truly effective, FPOs must engage in collaborative efforts with institutions and private entities. Such collaborations are instrumental in bridging resource gaps, whether they pertain to finances, information, technology, or any other crucial aspect of FPO operations

vi. **Building Collaboration with Institutions and Private Players:** It is imperative on the part of FPOs, to establish strategic collaborations with institutions such as APEDA, EXIM, academia and other government and private plyers for better understanding the dynamic international market environment. These collaborations help FPOs in mitigating unforeseen challenges that often arise during the initial stages of their life cycle. These type of collaborations helps FPOs to extend their support in the form of guidance, funding, technical assistance, latest research, foreign exchange fluctuations, forecasting services, innovation, trade opportunities, capacity building, etc.. to navigate the challenges effectively. Further collaborating with these institutions and industries, allows FPOs to better understand their inherent and unique challenges and in turn facilitates the creation of simplified regulatory environment that is more accommodating, streamlining the ease of doing.

Example: When it comes to exporting commodities to different countries, each nation has its own set of regulations and treatment protocols in place. Take, for example, mangoes exported to the United States; they must undergo an irradiation process. On the other hand, for exports to Japan and South Korea, mangoes undergo vapour heat treatment and hot water treatment to ensure the elimination of pests. These specialized treatment facilities are not widely available but are concentrated in just four locations across India: Gujarat Agro Industries Corporation Limited in Ahmedabad, Vashi (Navi Mumbai), Nasik, and Bengaluru.Establishing effective collaborations with these institutions proves to be highly beneficial for Farmer Producer Organizations (FPOs) (APEDA, 2023) Such partnerships grant FPOs access to these essential treatment facilities, allowing them to meet the stringent requirements of international markets whike streamlining the export processes.

vii. **Networking with Channel partners:** Streamlining the supply chain anomalies is a key factor in export success. Further for certain perishable products (mango, grapes, sea foods), the intensity of integration among the players play a key role in building high responsive supply chains. Consequently, forging connections with various channel partners, including third-party and fourth-party logistics service providers, becomes indispensable for optimizing channel efficiency and ensuring timely deliveries.Further collaborating with channel partners proves vital for meeting international quality standards, adhering to regulatory requirements, staying attuned to evolving market demands, and mitigating risks associated with market fluctuations.

    Example: In the case of seasonal agricultural commodities, seamless coordination among channel partners facilitates the exchange of information regarding ship carrier schedules, which must align precisely with harvesting schedules. Any lapse in information flow can severely impact export operations. Thus, networking with exporters, importers, certification agencies, and logistics providers fosters effective information exchange, shared infrastructure utilization, and ensures timely deliveries while optimizing overall channel efficiency.

viii. **Creating required infrastructure to meet the market needs:** While creating infrastructure, FPOs need to have a clear understanding of market requirements (quality standards and regulatory compliances), resource availability and its gap and ways to bridge the gap through collaborations. Failing to address these resource gaps could expose FPOs to substantial risks when entering the market.However, it's crucial to acknowledge that infrastructural necessities—such as cold storage, warehouses, processing facilities, transportation, and packaging—vary among FPOs. Therefore, FPOs must formulate a well-defined investment action plan tailored to their specific requirements. Concurrently, they should actively engage in establishing collaborations and fostering networks to ensure a holistic and effective approach to infrastructure development.

ix. **Linking FPOs to the value chain:** After understanding the international opportunities, FPO teams along with collaborated institutions and channel partners have to educate the member farmers in achieving the targeted produce with international quality and standards. Preparedness and understanding the needs of market by individual farmer, would reduce the FPO efforts to achieve the set goal through synergy. Once the products are identified, FPOs can access global markets with a minimum viable consignment and with a calculated risk. However, this requires a close integration among all players to achieve the ***proof of concept***.

    While accessing new markets, there is always an incubation period for market development. During this nascent period FPOs suffers financial burnouts. For example, consider the case of Shri Vilas Shinde, who prior to establishing Sahyadri Farmer Producer Company Ltd. (SFPCL), aimed to boost farmers' incomes by directly procuring grapes for export. Unfortunately, the entire grape consignment from India was rejected, resulting in a substantial loss of seven crores. Nevertheless, he personally compensated the losses incurred by the farmers. (Management Report, 2017-18). Likewise, all FPOs may encounter similar situations where their consignments face rejections during their initial phases because of iterating with new markets. Further, they might not have the capacity to absorb such losses without external support. Hence, the promoting and supporting agencies need to focus on fulfilling the financial burnouts during the initial scaling period through differential grants.

x. **Creating clusters to develop market driven ecosystem to gain competitive advantage:** Once theFPOsachieve successful proof of concept in linking themselves to international value chains, the experiences and learnings of these FPOs could be used by promoting agencies in nurturing and supporting other FPOs in the similar lines for creation of market driven ecosystems within identified geographical regions. Furthermore, FPOs dealing with similar commodities or related products, while having common infrastructural requirements, often operate in diverse geographical locations. These FPOs can be organized into clusters and federated, allowing them not only to develop tailored support schemes but also to gain a competitive edge in global markets. This collaboration fosters the sharing of knowledge, resources, and best practices among like-minded FPOs, resulting in collective growth and enhanced competitiveness on the international stage.

xi. **Redistribution of value created through community investments:** The value generated through this process should be reinvested in the community, supporting initiatives such as technology development or enhancing common resources, which may include infrastructure development and market facilities that further maximizing the benefits for FPOs.

xii. Competency Assessment – Need based Capacity Building: As evident from various reports, FPOs often lack competencies in various aspects. It's important to emphasize that capacity building for FPOs is an ongoing process, not a one-time endeavor. As FPOs advance through their life stages, it becomes crucial to conduct comprehensive competency assessments at various stages and address gaps through external interventions. Moreover, research indicates a positive correlation between competencies and business performance (Man et al., 2008; Esubalew & Raghurama, 2020). Additionally, skill development through capacity building is widely recognized as a critical factor in strengthening FPOs (Prasad, 2019). FPOs equipped with robust business skills tend to operate more effectively than those lacking such skills, as highlighted in recent studies (Singh, 2022). This underscores the significance of continuous competency enhancement to enhance the overall functionality and success of FPOs.

xiii.. Extending handholding till FPOs become viable and self-sustain: FPOs are farmer organizations formed by resource poor farmers to enhance theircollective strength. Yet, they lack capital, capacities, skills and other management capabilities. Therefore, it is crucial to nurture these FPOs from their inception in an incubation mode to till they evolve as potential social organizations. Similar to the "**Startup India**" initiative for entrepreneurship, FPOs also should receive continuous support, both financial and non-financial throughout their life cycle stages. Moreover, requirements of FPOs vary as they progress in their life stages. Consequently, it is essential to tailor support schemes to meet their specific needs rather than adopting generalized uniform approaches

Thus, by implementing tailored support schemes, incubation strategies, collaborative efforts, network building, and gradual resource pooling, the complex and varied challenges faced by FPOs can be more effectively addressed throughout their growth journey. This approach harnesses the full potential of FPOs, transforming them into viable and sustainable social organizations capable ofgeneratinghigher economic benefits to farmers

Conclusion

Farmer Producer Organizations (FPOs) play a vital role not only in building the capacities and skills of resource poor small farmers of India and as well improve their well being through providing access to output and input markets. In India, FPOs are engaged in both upstream and downstream activities. Upstream FPOs, focus on supplying agricultural inputs and services to members, while downstream FPOs market diverse agricultural products, facilitating sales to various markets for economic benefits. Participation in international markets, enhances FPOs business capacities, quality control measures, infrastructure investment, networkingand diversification, ultimately leading to economic growth and improved domestic markets. To effectively empower FPOs and enable their successful integration into international markets, a comprehensive approach is essential. This approach involves selecting competent managerial teams, conducting feasibility studies, understanding destination markets and risks, resource pooling, building collaborations with institutions and private players, networking with channel partners, creating necessary infrastructure, linking FPOs to value chains, reinvesting value in the community, continuous competency assessment, and providing sustained support throughout their life cycle, ultimately fostering their viability and economic impact.

References

Agricultural and Processed Food Products Export Development Authority (APEDA). (2023), Market News dated 20.02.2023. Retrieved from https://agriexchange.apeda.gov.in/news/Newssearch.aspx?newsid=48517&Date=20Feb2023

Esubalew, A. A., & Raghurama, A. (2020). The mediating effect of entrepreneurs' competencyon the relationship between bank finance and performance of micro, small, and medium enterprises (MSMEs). European Research on Management and Business Economics, 26(2): 87–95. https://doi.org/10.1016/j.iedeen.2020.03.001

Fischer, E., &Qaim, M. (2012). Linking smallholders to markets: Determinants and impacts of farmer collective action in Kenya. World Development, 40(6): 1255–1268. http://hdl.handle.net/10419/90498

Government of India (GOI). (2020). All India report on agriculture census, 2015-16. Department of Agriculture, Cooperation and Farmers Welfare, Ministry of Agriculture and Farmers Welfare, GOI, New Delhi.

Govil, R., Neti, A., & Rao, R. M. (2020). Farmer Producer Companies past, present and future, Azim Premji University, Bangalore

Latynskiy, E., &Berger, T. (2016). Networks of rural producer organizations in Uganda: What can be done to make them better. World Development, 78(1): 572-586.http://dx.doi.org/10.1016/j.worlddev.2015.10.014

Loeper, W. V., Musango, J. B., & Drimie, S. (2016). Analyzing challenges facing smallholders and conservation agriculture in South Africa: A system dynamics approach. South African Journal of Economic and Management Sciences, 19(5), 747-773. http://dx.doi.org/10.4102/sajems.v19i5.1588

Man T. W. Y., Lau T., & Snape E. (2008). Entrepreneurial competencies and the performance of small and medium enterprises: An investigation through a framework of competitiveness. Journal of Small Business and Entrepreneurship, 21(3), 257-276. https://doi.org/10.1080/08276331.2008.10593424

National Bank for Agricultural and Rural Development. (2015). Frequently asked questions on Farmer Producer Organizations, NABARD, Mumbai. Retrieved from https://www.nabard.org/demo/auth/writereaddata/File/FARMER%20PRODUCER%20ORGANISATIONS.pdf

National Bank for Agricultural and Rural Development. (2022).Handholding (Capacity building and Facilitation) of FPOs: Framework to implementation. Research Study 24, NABARD, Mumbai

Parthiban, S. R., Nain, M.S., Singh, R., Shivkumar., &Chahal, V.P. (2015). FPOs in reducing transaction costs: A study of Tamil Nadu Mango growers federation (TAMAFED). Indian Journal of Agricultural Sciences, 85(10): 55-59.http://dx.doi.org/10.56093/ijas.v85i10.52269

Pingali, P., Aiyar, A., Abraham, M., &Rahman, A. (2019). Linking Farms to Markets: Reducing Transaction Costs and Enhancing Bargaining Power. In: Transforming Food Systems for a Rising India. Palgrave Studies in Agricultural Economics and Food Policy. Palgrave Macmillan, Cham. https://doi.org/10.1007/978-3-030-14409-8_8

Prabhavathi, Y. (2022). A Study on Business Competencies and Performance Analysis Of FPOs Driven Agri Value Chains in the State Of Andhra Pradesh. Unpublished Ph.D (Thesis), University of Agricultural Sciences, Bangalore.

Prabhavathi, Y., Krishna Kishore, N.T., & Siddayya. (2023). Analysis of Collectivization of Small Holders in India: Competencies, Opportunities and Economic Impact. Journal of Community Mobilization and Sustainable Development. 18 (1): 146-152

Prasad, C. S. (2019). Farming as an enterprise: Ten years of FPO movement in India. State of livelihoods report, Access Development Services, New Delhi.(pp.37-48).

Shree, D.A.N., &Vaishnavi, P. (2022). Challenges faced by farmer producer organizations (FPOs): A review. Journal of Agricultural Extension Management, 23(1): 131-140

Singh, S. (2021b). Understanding performance and impact of producer companies: Cases studies across states and promoters in India. Centre for Management in Agriculture, Indian Institute of Management, Ahmedabad

Singh, S. (2022). How can India's farmer producer companies better serve small-scale farmers? International Institute of Environment and Development, London

Singh, S., & Singh, T. (2013). Producer companies in India – A study of organization and performance. CMA Publication No. 246, 1-126

Trebbin, A., &Hassler, M. (2012). Farmers' producer companies in India: a new concept for collective action. Environment and Planning A, 44(1): 411-427.http://dx.doi.org/10.1068/a44143

Vadivelu, A., &Kiran, B. (2013). Problems and prospects of agricultural marketing in India: An overview. International Journal of Agricultural and Food Science, 3(3): 108-118. https://api.semanticscholar.org/CorpusID:4864110

10

Trends and Potential of Fresh and Dried Grapes Exports from India

Gurindapalli Swetha[1] and Ritambhara Singh[2]

[1]Department of Agricultural Economics, Post Graduate College of Agriculture, Dr. Rajendra Prasad Central Agricultural University Pusa, Samastipur, Bihar
[2]School of Agribusiness and Rural Management, Dr. Rajendra Prasad Central Agricultural University, Pusa, Samastipur, Bihar

Abstract

India's grape industry has emerged as a key contributor to horticultural exports, driven by increasing production, evolving market strategies, and trade liberalization. This chapter analyses the trends, growth, instability, and export potential of both fresh (HS 080610) and dried grapes (HS 080620) from India between 2004 and 2023. While, India ranks among the top global producers, the fresh grape segment has seen consistent growth in exports, supported by initiatives like APEDA's GrapeNet traceability system and private-sector innovation through companies like Sahyadri Farms and Mahindra Agri. In contrast, the dried grape segment, despite high growth potential, has faced volatility and continues to show a trade deficit. Using compound growth rates (CGR) and the Cuddy-Della Valle Index (CDVI), the study evaluates performance across production, trade value, and instability metrics. Exports potential maps highlight untapped markets such as the United States, EU, and Southeast Asia. Strengthening post-harvest infrastructure, ensuring compliance with international quality standard, and investing in value addition remain critical for India to enhance its global competitiveness in grape exports.

Keyword: *Fresh grapes, Dried grapes, Export Potential, GrapeNet, Growth and instability*

Introduction

Grapes are one of India's most popular fruits due to their sweet flavor and versatility. Grapes can be consumed as fresh or dried fruit and used for making jam, juice, jelly, vinegar, wine, grape seed extracts and grape seed oil. Approximately 71% of world grape production is used for wine, 27% as fresh fruit, and 2% as dried fruit. However, in India, 90% of grapes are used for table purpose, even though wine making has made strides. The rest of the grape is used mostly for raisins (Venkitasamy *et al.*, 2019). Grape exports from India started in 1991 with the initiation of economic liberalisation (Thulasiram and Alagumani, 2015). India exports 3.4% of the world's grapes, ranking 11th globally with an export concentration of 0.14 (ITC,2024).

According to the National Horticulture Board (2010), India's fresh fruit exports have grown significantly over the past two decades, with the quantity increasing more than fourfold and the value increasing tenfold. The major exported fruits are mangoes with 74,460 tonnes and grapes with 117,670 tonnes and both have contributed significantly to India's foreign exchange earnings. Despite being the world's ninth-largest producer, India has significant potential to earn foreign exchange through grape exports (Nithin, 2016). The comparative advantage of various fruit and vegetable products emphasizes the need for the country to focus on commodity-specific strategies to tap their export potential (Raman et al., 2023). The International Trade Center identified fresh grapes (080610) and dried grapes (080620) as India's top export potential products in the fruit category, ranking first and sixth respectively. The United Nations Economic and Social Commission for Asia and the Pacific states that agricultural trade is crucial for the sustainable economic growth of developing and least developed countries in Asia. The growing demand for fresh fruits, cut flowers, and plants in the European union, Japan, and North America opens up new export opportunities (UN-ESCAP, 2015). There is a need to expand into new markets and explore new consumer groups with varying income levels in both developed and developing countries (Singh, & Khanna, 2021).

The world area and production of grapes were 6,595,680 ha and 72,486,522 tons, respectively, in 2023. Global table grape production for 2024-25 is projected to increase by nearly 1.0 million tons to 28.9 million, with higher output in China and India (USDA, 2024). The world major grape producers are China, Italy, France, USA, Spain, India,Turkiye and Chile.The area and production of grapes in India were 1,69,000 ha and 3,740,000 tons, respectively in 2023 (FAOSTAT database). Grape cultivation covered 2.5% of the India's total fruit-producing area and the major grape growing states are Maharashtra, Karnataka, Tamil Nadu, and Mizoram (APEDA, 2024).

The world export of fresh grapes in terms of quantity and value are 45,94,906 tons and 94,14,979 USD respectively, in 2023. The world major fresh grape exporters are Peru, Chile, China, Italy, South Africa, Netherland, India and

USA. The world export of dried grapes in terms of quantity and value was 850,478 tons and 1,756,377 USD respectively in 2023. The world major dried grape exporters are Turkiye, Iran, Chile, Uzbekistan, South Africa, USA, India and China (ITC database). World trade for grapes is about 4.9 million tons and the contribution of India is about 2.98 percent (FAO, 2016). Grapes are one of India's important fruit exports, with a 9.1 percent share in all fruit and nut exports (Sharma and Jain, 2011). The export of fresh grapes from India in terms of quantity and value was 2,84,269 tons and 3,29,851 USD respectively in 2023. The major destinations for fresh grape exports are Netherland, United Kingdom, UAE, Bangladesh and Russia. The export of dried grapes from India in terms of quantity and value was 42,014 tons and 54,014 USD respectively in 2023. The major destinations for dried grape exports are Morocco, Romania, Russia, Saudi Arabia and Vietnam. The WTO agreements and trade liberalization have significantly boosted Indian grape exports. APEDA has started a training program for horticulture producers of specific fruits like grapes, mangoes, litchis, and Kinnows in selected areas. It is also working to extend the shelf life of these fruits using controlled/ modified atmosphere storage and refrigerated containers for sea transport. Additionally, APEDA has created pre-harvest manuals for various fruits and vegetables to help farmers and producers improve quality (Kumar and Mittal, 2003). Additionally, interventions by the Central and State Governments, Mahagrapes, and NAFED have played a crucial role in enhancing the export of high-quality Indian grapes (Kumar and Devraj, 2020). This study aims to examine fresh and dried grapes by analyzing their growth rate, instability, trends, and export potential markets.The study will identify key markets and formulate the strategies to increase the export potential of fresh and dried grapes to enhance India's trade performance.

Methodology

The data on grape products exports from India over a period of 20 years from 2004 to 2023 was collected from Food and Agriculture Organization Statistics (FAOSTAT), International Trade Centre (ITC). According to the Harmonized System of the World Customs Organization, grapes are classified under chapter 8 – "Edible fruit and nuts; peel of citrus fruits or melons" and Heading 0806 "Fresh or dried grapes". The details of specific subheadings (Hs 6-digit code level) included in this study are given below (Nisar *et al.*, 2020).

- Hs 6-digit code 080610: Fresh Grapes
- Hs 6-digit code 080620: Dried Grapes

I. Estimation of Growth Rate

The growth of grape products in terms of area, production, export quantity, export value, unit value, import quantity and import value was estimated using Compound Growth Rate (CGR).

$$\mathbf{Y = ab^x}$$

Where,

Y – Value of India's grape products

x – Time period (in years)

a – Constant

b – Coefficient value

CGR (%) = (Antilog 'b' - 1) x 100

The growth rates of grape products are classified into three ranges namely as Low growth rate (between 0 to 5), Medium growth rate (greater than 5 and up to 10) and High growth rate (greater than 10) (Das *et.al*, 2016; Vasavada and Shiyani, 2023).

Estimation of Instability

The Cuddy-Della Valle Index (CDVI) is a measurement tool used to gauge the degree of instability in time series data by accounting for trends. It's calculated by multiplying the coefficient of variation with the square root of one minus the adjusted R-squared value of the best-fitted model.

Cuddy-Della Valle Index

$$\mathbf{I = CV^* \sqrt{1 - AdjR^2}}$$

CV = Standard deviation/Mean*100

Where,

I = Cuddy Della Valle index of instability (%),

CV = coefficient of variation (%)

Adjusted R^2 = adjusted coefficient of determination.

The instability of grape products is classified into three ranges namely as, Low instability (between 0 to 15), Medium instability (between 15 to 30) and High instability (greater than 30) (Sihmar, 2014).

Results and Discussion

World Scenario of Grapes

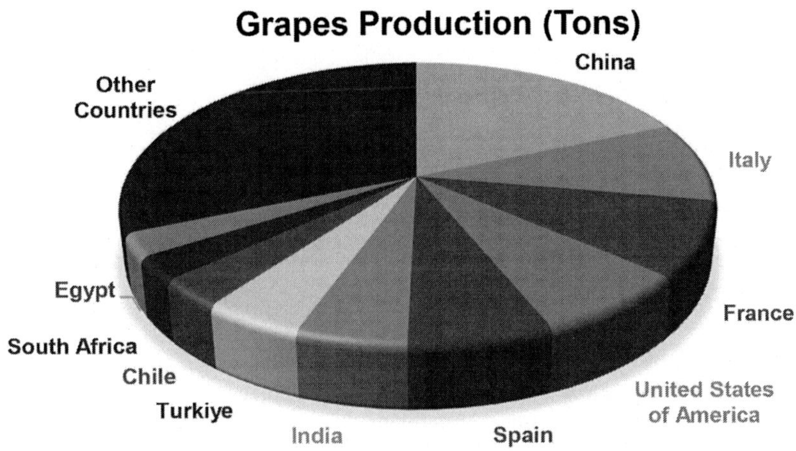

Fig. 1: World major producers of grapes (2023)

The world's grape production in 2023 was 72.49 million tons, with China leading at 13.5 million tons (Mamta Saxena, 2014), followed by Italy at 6.67 million tons, and India secured sixth position with 3.74 million tons of production. The top 10 producers are China (18.62%), Italy (9.20%), France (8.56%), USA (7.40%), Spain (6.65%), India (5.16%), Turkey (4.69%), Chile (3.20%), South Africa (2.72%), and Egypt (2.65%). These top 10 countries contributed 68.86% of the world's total production, highlighting their significant impact on the global market. The other countries produced 22,569,482 tons accounting for 31.14% of world's production.

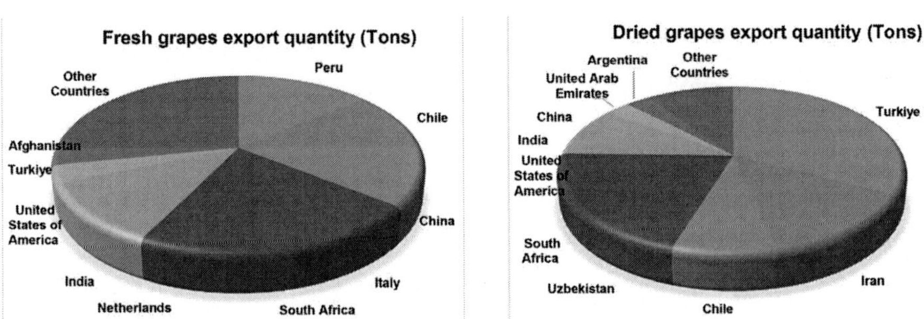

Fig. 2: World major grapes exporters in terms of export quantity (2023)

The world export quantity of fresh grapes (080610) was 45.95 million tons in 2023. Peru was the top exporter with 647,531 tons, followed by Chile with 503,937 tons and India secured seventh position with 284,269 tons of export quantity. The top ten exporters of fresh grapes (fig.2) are Peru (14.09%), Chile (10.97%), China (10.52%), Italy (8.42%), South Africa (6.92%), Netherlands (6.47%), India (6.19%), USA (5.18%), Turkey (3.19%), and Afghanistan (3.10%). The other countries contributed 1,146,385 tons of export quantity and accounting for 24.95% of world export.

The world export quantity of dried grapes (080620) was 850,478 tons in 2023. Turkiye was the top exporter with 277,081 tons, followed by Iran with 119,358 tons and India secured seventh position with 42,014 tons of export quantity. The top ten exporters of dried grapes (fig.2) are Turkiye (32.58%), Iran (14.03%), Chile (8.35%), Uzbekistan (7.76%), South Africa (6.73%), USA (6.03%), India (4.94%), China (4.66%), the United Arab Emirates (2.68%), Argentina (2.61%). The other countries contributed 81,874 tons of export quantity and accounting for 9.63% of world's export.

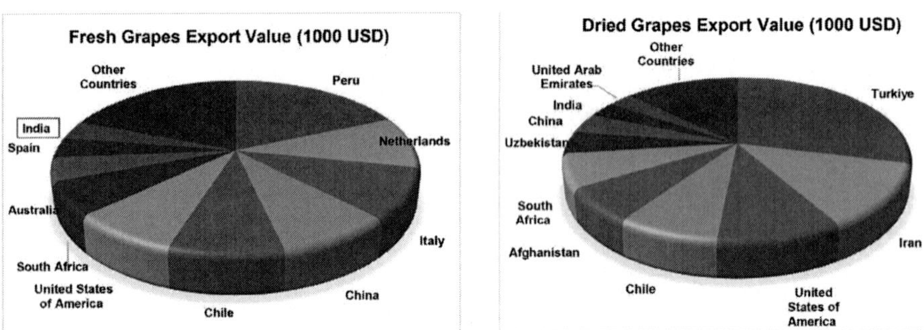

Fig. 3: World major grapes exporters in terms of export value (2023)

The world export value of fresh grapes (080610) was 94,14,979 USD in 2023. Peru was the top exporter with an export value of 1,745,479 USD, followed by the Netherlands with 914,398 USD and India secured tenth position with 329,851 USD of export value. The top 10 exporters of fresh grapes (fig 3) are Peru (18.54%), Netherlands (9.71%), Italy (9.48%), China (8.64%), Chile (8.62%), USA (8.16%), South Africa (6.36%), Australia (4.25%), Spain (3.77%) and India (3.50%). The other countries contributed 17,86,043 USD of export value and accounting for 18.97% of the world's export.

The world export value of dried grapes (080620) was 1,756,377 USD in 2023. Turkey was the top exporter with an export value of 508,209 USD, followed by Iran with 222,827 USD and India secured ninth position with 54,014 USD of export value. The top ten exporters of dried grapes (fig.3) are Turkiye

(28.94%), Iran (12.69%), USA (9.94%), Chile (8.13%), Afghanistan (6.84%), South Africa (6.60%), Uzbekistan (4.41%), China (3.94%), India (3.08%), and United Arab Emirates (2.71%). The other countries contributed 223,446 USD of export value and accounting for 12.72% of the world's export.

Scenario of Grapes products from India

The figure 4 represents the status of India's grape industry from 2004-2023 reveals significant growth across production, consumption, and exports. The production of grapes has shown a consistent upward trajectory over the period, increasing from 1,474,800 tons in 2004 to 3,740,000 tons in 2023 due to good soil moisture from the monsoon and better farming techniques (USDA, 2024). However, notable dip was observed around 2010, where production temporarily decreased to about 1 million tons. Grape cultivation offers high returns per unit area, but the expansion is slow due to high initial vineyard costs and recurring production expenses. Additionally, the risk of crop loss from unexpected weather changes is significant (Shikhamany, n.d.). The consumption pattern closely mirrors the production trend but maintains a slight gap below production levels. Domestic consumption has grown from 3,455,731 tons in 2004 to 1,452,017 tons in 2023, indicating a strong domestic market for grapes. In India around 26% of fresh grapes are turned into raisins, 1.5% for wine, 0.5% for juice, and the rest are consumed as fresh fruit and gaining popularity due to their health benefits (Somkuwar et al., 2019). At the same time, India accounts for nearly one percent of the world's fresh fruit export and around two percent of the world's processed fruits and juices. Increased population, rising standard of living, and higher domestic demand for fruits could be reasons for lower export from India (Renjini, 2024).

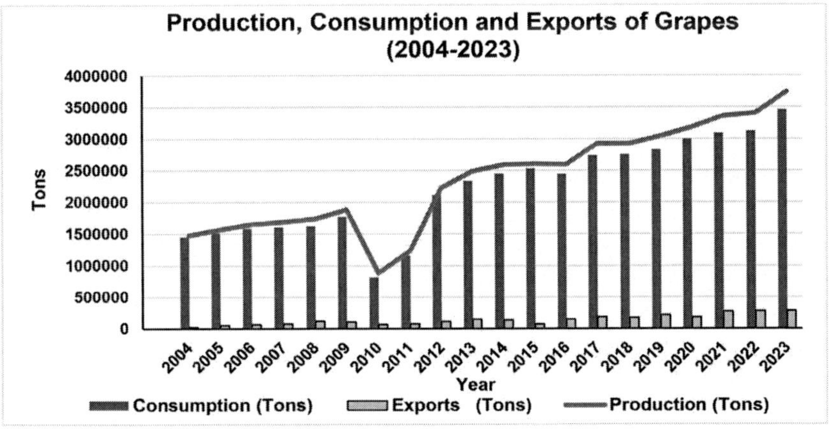

Fig. 4: Production, Consumption and Exports of India's Grapes (2004-2023)

The exports showed relatively modest volumes compared to production and consumption but demonstrated a gradual increase over the years. Exports have grown from 22,783 tons in 2004 to approximately 284269 tons by 2023, suggesting India's growing presence in the international grape market. In total fruit production, grapes made up only three percent, but they accounted for the largest share (46.86%) of export earnings, amounting to US $315.48 million in the fresh fruit category during the TE 2020-21(Renjini, 2024). India has a great scope to increase the domestic production and thereby export of grapes in large quantities (Thulasiram and Alagumani, 2015).

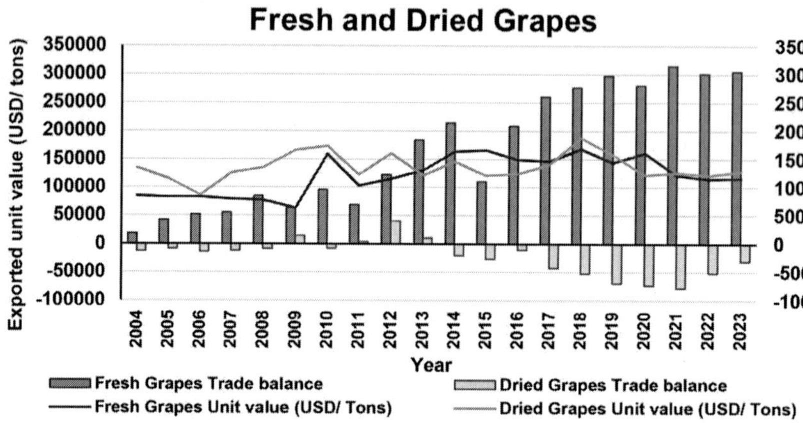

Fig. 5: Trade balance and export unit value of India's Grapes (2004-2023)

The India's grapes trade in figure 5 revealed distinct patterns for fresh grapes (080610) and dried grapes (080620) during the period 2004 to 2023. Fresh grape exports demonstrated a positive trade balance throughout the period, with significant growth in the trade surplus from 18,192 USD in 2004 to 3,05587 USD by 2023. The unit value for fresh grapes remained relatively stable, fluctuating between 1,000-1,500 USD/ton, but was low compared to dried grapes export value because Indian fruits are exported to low-value markets because they do not meet the hygiene, labeling, and pesticide residue standards of developed countries (Renjini, 2024). Dried grapes showed a negative trade balance across most of the period, suggesting India is a net importer of dried grapes. The processing of this fruit in our country is very limited as compared to the traditional grape growing countries in the world where more than 80 percent of the produce is processed in the form of wine, raisin and juice (Sharma and Adulse, 2007). India is expected to be a major importer of dried grapes in the next five years. It shows a high value in terms of quantity and percentage which is more than 50 percent of all Afghanistan's dried grapes export (Mushair *et al.*, 2020). The unit value for dried grapes exhibited more volatility and higher values compared to fresh grapes, ranging from about 1,000 to 1,800 USD/ton, with notable peaks and subsequent stabilization. The investment in raisin grape production is significantly lower than in table grape production for export, raisin exporters are likely to achieve better price realization due to a superior cost-benefit ratio (Sharma and Adulse, 2007).

The divergent trends between fresh and dried grapes highlight India's stronger competitive position in fresh grape exports while remaining dependent on imports for dried grapes. The positive trade balance in fresh grapes indicates successful market penetration and competitive advantage in international markets, whereas the persistent negative trade balance in dried grapes. The imports of processed fruit products is on the rise because of rapid explosion of middle class population and the sharp increase in the disposable income of this segment. Moreover people at large are becoming health conscious and are switching to rich nutritious food from traditional food grains. This further implies that the domestic demand for processed fruit products is increasing, and Indian fruit processors should now focus on meeting the needs of this upcoming buoyant segment (Bung, 2012).

The table1, results revealed India's share in the global grape industry from 2004 to 2023, showing significant growth across area, production and exports. India's share in world grape cultivation area increased substantially from 0.79% in 2004 to 2.56% in 2023, indicating expanded farming operations. Similarly, the country's share in global production grew from 2.19% to 5.16%, demonstrating improved productivity and yield management. The fresh grapes sector in India made remarkable progress, with its share in world export quantity rising from 0.74% to 6.19%, while its share in world export value increased from 0.59% to 3.50% between 2004 and 2023. India's share in world dried grape export quantity raised from 0.07% in 2004 to 4.94% by 2023 and peaking at 4.13% in 2013. The export value share of dried grapes followed a similar pattern, rising from 0.09% in 2004 to 3.08% in 2023. Before 1994-95, only small quantities of fruits and vegetables were exported. Since the establishment of the World Trade Organization, international trade in fruits and vegetables has increased rapidly compared to other agricultural commodities. Pomegranates, Grapes, Bananas, Mangos, and Citrus fruits were most exported fruits from India (Suman et al., 2022). Therefore, India's transformation into a more significant player in the global grape industry, particularly in fresh grape exports, though there remains potential for further value addition and market development in the dried grapes sector.

Table 1: India's share % in world area, production and exports of grapes (2004–2023)

Year	Share % in world area (hectares)	Share % in world production (Tons)	Fresh Grapes (080610)		Dried Grapes (080620)	
			Share % in world export quantity (Tons)	Share % in world export value (1000USD)	Share % in world export quantity (Tons)	Share % in world export value (1000USD)
2004	0.79	2.19	0.74	0.59	0.07	0.09
2005	0.83	2.34	1.49	1.08	0.04	0.04
2006	0.90	2.46	1.87	1.28	0.04	0.03
2007	0.90	2.55	2.12	1.27	0.02	0.01
2008	0.96	2.61	3.15	1.58	0.42	0.32
2009	1.13	2.78	2.91	1.27	1.93	1.82
2010	1.52	1.32	1.71	1.75	0.45	0.38
2011	1.60	1.79	1.89	1.19	1.26	0.62
2012	1.68	3.22	2.83	1.95	3.94	2.62
2013	1.68	3.25	3.52	2.62	4.13	2.13
2014	1.69	3.50	3.27	2.91	1.86	1.18
2015	1.69	3.40	1.76	1.67	2.57	1.50
2016	1.77	3.48	3.31	2.94	3.97	2.49
2017	2.00	3.97	3.86	3.33	2.76	2.16
2018	2.02	3.65	3.66	3.47	2.52	2.39
2019	2.02	3.94	4.55	3.65	2.64	1.96
2020	2.18	4.14	3.74	3.12	2.66	1.67
2021	2.29	4.37	5.08	3.50	2.15	1.47
2022	2.42	4.35	5.60	3.29	3.07	2.00
2023	2.56	5.16	6.19	3.50	4.94	3.08

Source: Authors' computations based on FAO and ITC Database

Trends of Grape products from India

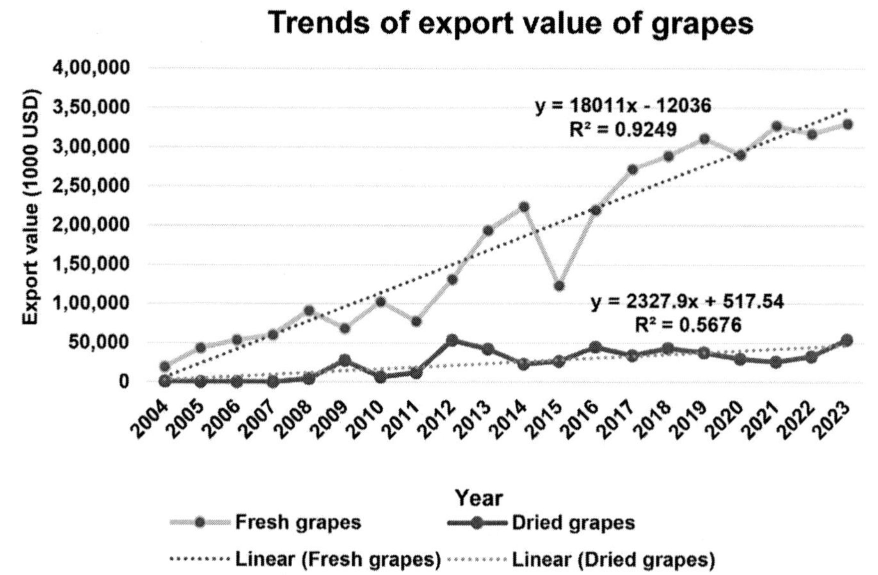

Fig. 8: Trends of export value of India's Grapes (2004-2023)

The trends of grape exports for fresh grapes (080610) and dried grapes (080620) exports from 2004 to 2023 are represented in figure 8. Fresh grapes export value demonstrated remarkable growth over the period, with values increasing from 19271 USD in 2004 to 329851 USD by 2023. Thc data shows several notable phases in fresh grape exports initially moderate growth from 2004 to 2011, followed by accelerated growth from 2012 to 2014. A significant dip occurred in 2015, but the market quickly recovered and resumed its upward trajectory. The export of fresh grapes from India in quantity, value in US dollars and value in rupees have been continuously increasing at a good pace having little bit ups and downs (Chetia *et al*, 2022). This strong upward trend is confirmed by the high R^2 value of 92.49 and the linear equation shows an average annual increase of 18,011 USD in fresh grapes exports. In contrast, dried grape exports followed a more modest and volatile pattern indicated by lower R^2 value of 56.76. The dried grapes trend line equation indicates an average annual increase of 2,328 USD, significantly lower than fresh grapes. Dried grapes export showed minor fluctuations throughout the period, maintaining values generally below 50,000 USD. The stark difference in export values suggests that fresh grapes have benefited more from market developments, improved logistics, and international demand, while dried grapes maintained a stable but limited market presence.

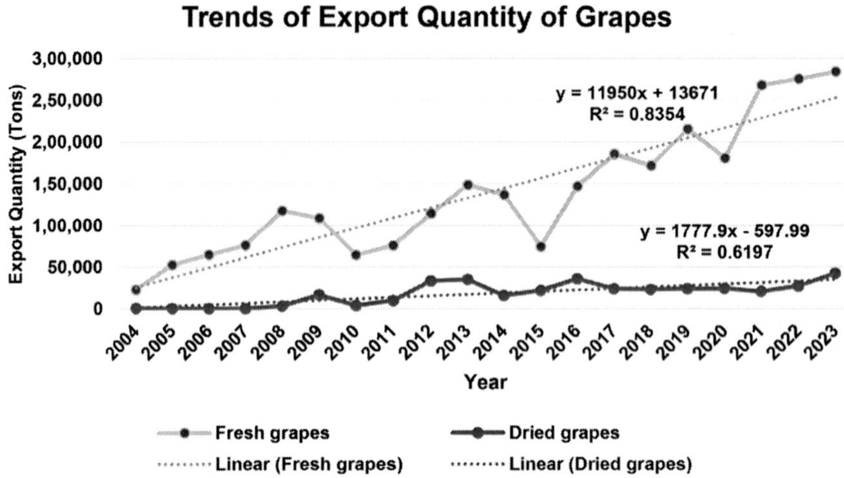

Fig. 9: Trends of export value of India's Grapes (2004-2023)

Trends for the export quantities of fresh grapes (080610) and dried grapes (080620) over the past two decades(2004 to 2023) are represented in figure 9. Fresh grapes export quantity experienced steady growth, increasing from 22,783 tons in 2004 to 2,84,269 tons by 2023. This growth is demonstrated by the trend line equation shows an average annual increase of 11,950 tons in fresh grapes export quantity with an R^2 value of 83.64, indicating a strong fit. Overall, the growing export quantities of fresh grapes underscore a burgeoning demand, driven by their appeal and diverse utility in fresh consumption markets worldwide. Dried grapes export quantity showed more fluctuations but an increasing trend. Dried grapes export quantity have risen from 529 tons to 42,014 tons over the study period, following the trend line equation which shows an average annual increase of 1777 tons in dried grapes export with an R^2 value of 61.97. The results revealed that grape exports, both fresh and dried, have seen substantial increases over the study period, with fresh grapes experiencing more rapid and stable growth compared to dried grapes.

Growth and Instability of Grapes product from India

The table 2 represents the Growth and instability patterns of the India's grapes sector from 2004 to 2023. The results demonstrated moderate but stable growth in the area and production of grapes. The area under grapes cultivation demonstrated a medium growth rate with a CGR of 5.89% and low instability (CDVI of 6.46%), indicating a steady and reliable expansion of cultivation area. Similarly, production exhibited a medium growth rate of 5.61% CGR with relatively low instability (CDVI of 14.55%), suggesting consistent and sustainable production patterns over the study period. Fresh grapes sector export performance has been notably strong, with export quantities showing a high growth rate of 10.18% CGR, accompanied by an even higher growth in export value at 13.97% CGR and showing medium levels of instability with CDVI values of 23.17% and 17.62% respectively. Exports are expected to rise by over 20,000 tons to 335,000, aided by the Indian rupee's depreciation, aiding exports to neighboring countries and the EU (USDA, 2024). The unit value growth was relatively modest at 3.44% CGR with medium instability (CDVI of 23.13%), suggesting moderate price fluctuations. Import patterns for fresh grapes showed high growth rates for both quantity (11.97% CGR) and value (12.23% CGR), but with notably high instability in quantities (CDVI of 45.13%) and medium instability in values (CDVI of 25.91%), indicating volatile import patterns. The dried grapes sector exhibited remarkably high growth rates but with significant instability. The export quantities and values showed exceptional growth rates of 28.41% and 29.03% CGR, but these were accompanied by high instability indices of CDVI at 46.85% and 49.48% respectively. This suggests that while the sector has expanded rapidly, it has experienced substantial fluctuations. The CGR of unit value (0.48%) showed very low growth rate compared to fresh grapes and medium instability of CDVI at 17.70%. The relatively stable unit values for fresh grapes compared to dried grapes also indicates a more mature and established market for fresh grape exports. The results of dried grapes imports revealed medium growth in quantities (8.48% CGR) but high growth in values (15.82% CGR), both experiencing medium to high instability of CDVI at 24.06% and 33.85% respectively.

The area and production exhibit a medium growth rate and low instability. This indicates a stable increase in the land area and productivity over the observed period with minimal fluctuations in growth rates. Fresh grapes unit value portrayed a low growth rate, while the export quantity, export value, import quantity, and import value experienced high growth rate. There was medium instability for export quantity, export value, unit value and import value. Dried Grapes unit value showed a low growth rate, whereas import quantity registered a medium growth rate. The dried grapes also exhibited high growth rate for export quantity, export value, and import value like fresh grapes. Increased globalization and liberalization of markets are opening new export markets for Indian fresh and processed products, especially high-value agricultural products such as fruits (Umali and Sur, 2007).

Table 2: Growth and Instability of Grapes from India (2004-05 to 2023-24)

	Area (Hectares)	Production (Tons)	Fresh Grapes (080610)					Dried Grapes (080620)				
			Export Quantity (Tons)	Export value (1000 USD)	Unit value (USD/ Tons)	Import Quantity (Tons)	Import value (1000 USD)	Export Quantity (Tons)	Export value (1000 USD)	Unit value (USD/ Tons)	Import Quantity (Tons)	Import value (1000 USD)
CGR (%)	5.89	5.61	10.18	13.97	3.44	11.97	12.23	28.41	29.03	0.48	8.48	15.82
C.V (%)	31.69	34.27	55.59	62.57	28.59	78.46	57.25	73.94	73.24	17.39	53.77	79.24
CDVI (%)	6.46	14.55	23.17	17.62	23.13	45.13	25.91	46.85	49.48	17.70	24.06	33.85

Source: Authors' computations based on FAO and ITC Database

Note : CGR - Compound Growth Rate, CV- Coefficient of variation (%), CDVI- Cuddy Della Vella Index (%)

Table 3: Classification of Growth rate and Instability of Grapes from India

Category	**CGR- Compound Growth Rate (%)**			**CDVI - Cuddy Della Vella Index (%)**		
	Low growth rate CGR ranges: (0 to 5)	**Medium growth rate CGR ranges: (>5 to10)**	**High growth rate CGR ranges: (>10)**	**Low instability CDVI ranges: (0 to 15)**	**Medium instability CDVI ranges: (15 to 30)**	**High instability CDVI ranges: (>30)**
Grapes	-	Area, Production	-	Area, Production	-	-
Fresh grapes (080610)	Unit value	-	Export quantity, Export value, Import quantity, Import value	-	Export quantity, Export value, Unit value, Import value	-
Dried grapes (080620)	Unit value	Import quantity	Export quantity, Export value, Import value	-	Unit value, Import quantity	Export quantity, Export value, Import value

There was medium instability for unit value and import quantity, while the export quantity, export value and import value experienced high instability. The instability in exports is also caused by the stringent quality requirements imposed by other countries (USAID-CHAMP, 2016).

Export potential map of Grapes from India

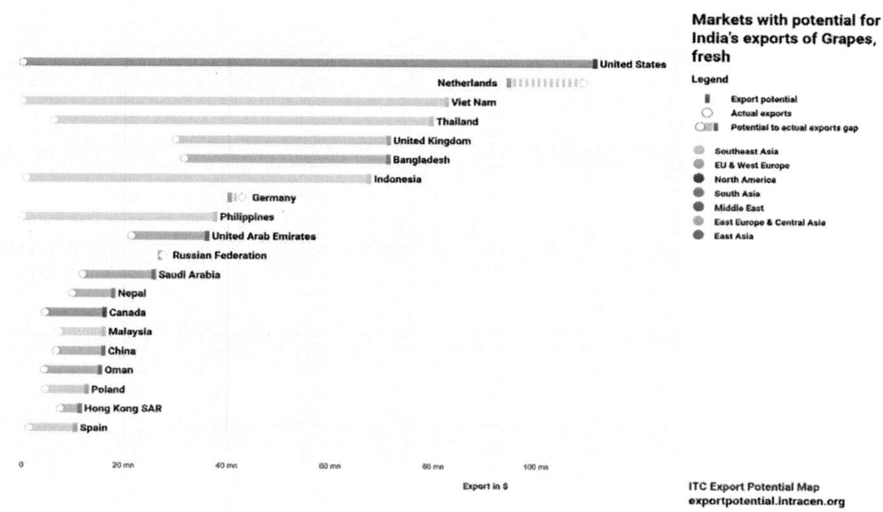

Fig. 10: Export potential map of Fresh grapes (080610) from India as sourced from ITC

The product with greatest export potential from India to world under fruit category is fresh grapes (080610), among all fruits showed the largest unrealized potential. The absolute difference between export potential (969 million USD) and actual exports (374 million USD) in value terms, leaving room to realize additional exports worth 623 million USD. The countries with greatest potential for India's exports of fresh grapes (080610) are United States, Netherlands, Viet Nam, Thailand and UK. Indian fresh grapes are exported to more than 50 countries, exports are mainly concentrated in the Netherlands, Bangladesh, United Kingdom and United Arab Emirates (Chetia *et al*, 2022). USA showed the largest absolute difference between export potential and actual exports in value terms, leaving room to realize additional exports worth 110 million USD. As the grape harvest arrives in April, India can take advantage of its early entry into the USA market and supply grapes to wine manufacturers (APEDA, 2020a,b). The regions with greatest potential for India's exports of fresh grapes (080610) are Southeast Asia, EU & West Europe and North America. Southeast Asia shows the largest absolute difference between export potential and actual exports in value terms, leaving room to realize additional exports worth $273 million USD. India's major importing partners for most of the horticultural products are Asian and Middle East countries. The unit price realization from horticultural exports to these countries was much lower compared to the European countries, USA and Japan (Idris et al., 2015). High dependence on one or two export markets would increase the trade risk in the long run. There is a need to diversify the geographical concentration (Chetia *et al*, 2022).

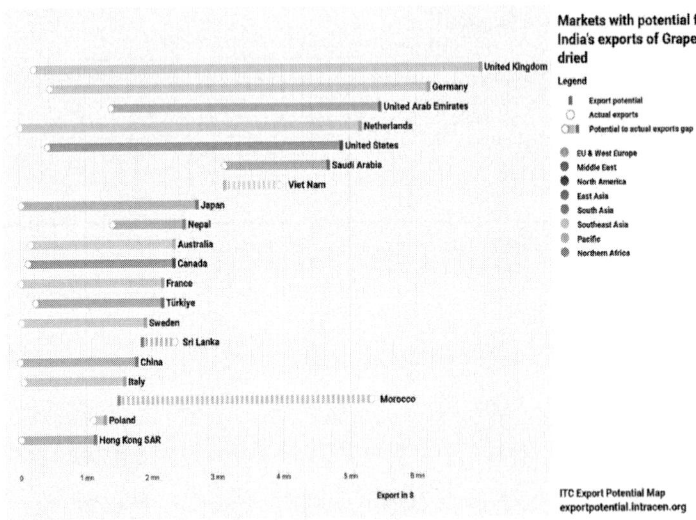

Fig. 11: Export potential map of Dried grapes (080620) from India as sourced from ITC

The products with greatest export potential from India to world are dried grapes (080620), among all fruits showed the largest absolute difference between export potential (81 million USD) and actual exports (38 million USD) in value terms, leaving room to realize additional exports worth 58 million USD. The countries with greatest potential for India's exports of dried grapes (080620) are United Kingdom, Germany, United Arab Emirates, Netherlands and USA. United Kingdom shows the largest absolute difference between potential and actual exports in value terms, leaving room to realize additional exports worth 6.7 million USD. The regions with greatest potential for India's exports of dried grapes (080620) are Europe Union, West Europe, Middle East and North America. Europe union and West Europe shows the largest absolute difference between export potential and actual exports in value terms, leaving room to realize additional exports worth 28 million USD. India's horticultural trade stands out when compared with its key competitors in North American, Asian, and European markets, as against China, Malaysia, Thailand, and Indonesia. Studies indicate that India holds a competitive edge over its main competitors, especially in the EU markets, for vegetables and fruits but not for flowers (Bhattacharyya, 2011). Hence, shipping fresh fruits and vegetables are gradually becoming challenging but exporting their processed variants is easier. The primary drivers of the industry for fruit and vegetable processing are a rise in consumer concerns about the safety of food products and demand for processed quality food items (Kearney, 2010).

Apeda's Grapenet

Grape Net emerged as a pioneering solution in response to a major crisis that threatened India's grape export sector in the mid-2000s. The industry faced potential ban from European markets due to pesticide residue issues, with consignments being held at ports and exporters suffering significant financial losses. Indian exporters are not able to comply with the food safety and health standards imposed by developed countries like the European Union and the United States of America (Das 2008, Goyal et al. 2017; Mukherjee et al. 2019). To improve the safety and quality of fruit and vegetable products which are essential to daily diets. It is crucial to establish a robust traceability system for agricultural products. This can be achieved by leveraging advanced technology to mark and record the production, processing, and circulation information of fruit and vegetable products. Such a system will enable product traceability, thereby enhancing product transparency and credibility (Tong et al., 2023). To address this challenge, the Agricultural and Processed Food Products Export Development Authority (APEDA) developed Grape Net during 2006-08, establishing India's first comprehensive traceability system. Grape Net functions as an internet-based certification and traceability software system that monitors every aspect of grape exports from India to the European Union. Its comprehensive approach ensures that no documentation can be issued without going through the software, enabling complete traceability from retail shelves back to the specific farm plot. In February 2021, APEDA significantly enhanced the system by incorporating cloud migration and blockchain technology, known as APEDA Trust Chain, which provided additional layers of security and data authenticity.

The implementation process began with establishing a robust regulatory framework, including clear Government of India regulations and procedures for all stakeholders. This was followed by the development of a centralized web-based monitoring software that integrated all participants in the grape export supply chain. The system successfully brought together over 40,000 farmers, more than 100 packing houses and exporters, multiple testing laboratories, and various government departments under a single platform. India cultivates grapes on 140,000 hectares, producing 3.4 million metric tonnes annually, mainly in Maharashtra, Telangana, and Karnataka. In 2019-20, India exported 1,93,690 metric tonnes of fresh grapes worth Rs 2,177 crore and the major destinations are Netherlands, Russia, the UK, Bangladesh, the UAE, and Saudi Arabia.

The impact of GrapeNet has been substantial, as evidenced by its successful monitoring of all grape consignments to the EU since 2007. The system's effectiveness was recognized through the National E-governance Award (GOLD) in 2007-08 and the eASIA award in 2009. The success of GrapeNet has inspired similar initiatives for other agricultural products, including Peanut.Net for peanut products, Tracenet for organic products, and Meat. Net for buffalo meat. APEDA is now exploring the integration of AI-based data mining solutions to build forecasting systems for exports. The system's innovative approach to ensuring food safety and quality has not only saved India's grape export industry but has also established a model for agricultural export traceability that combines regulatory compliance, technological innovation, and stakeholder collaboration. The 'Grape Net' service by APEDA helps stakeholders test and certify grapes for export to the European Union, ensuring compliance with standards. This service has boosted exports, as Indian grapes are highly demanded in the EU due to their good returns, despite strict quality requirements (E.I.B.O, 2014).

Case Studies of Grape Exporters from India

Case Study 1: Sahyadri Farms

Sahyadri Farms emerged as a remarkable success story in India's agricultural sector. In 2003, Sahyadri started as a privately held company with 10 marginal farmers as farmer entrepreneurs. In 2004, it shipped 4 containers of grapes to Europe.3 By 2010, the number increased to 140 farmers and the company shipped 150 containers (Lalita, 2019). Under the leadership of Vilas Shinde, the organization transformed into a Farmer Producer Company (FPC) in 2011, creating a unique hybrid model between a cooperative and a private enterprise. Though SFPCL is working with a variety of horticultural products, we specifically focus on grapes, with which the SFPCL started first. At all India level, grapes occupy a premier position in exports with 232.9 thousand tonnes valued at Rs. 2,08,835 lakhs (GOI, 2017). Sahyadri has exported 1,459 containers around 22 thousand tonnes of grapes to various world markets this season from 2018 to 2019. By 2022, Sahyadri Farms had grown exponentially to become India's largest grape exporter, surpassing established players like Mahindra Agri and achieving revenues of nearly Rs 800 crore. Their success is built on a foundation of over 18,000 registered farmers cultivating across

31,000 acres, with about 1,500 farmers specifically dedicated to grape cultivation, producing more than 20,000 tonnes of fresh grapes on over 5,000 acres.

The impact on farmer income has been substantial, with many grape farmers in the Nashik region earning over Rs 1 crore annually. This success is particularly noteworthy given the traditional challenges faced by small farmers in India's agricultural economy. The company has shown remarkable adaptability to market challenges, as demonstrated during recent shipping disruptions in the Red Sea. Despite increased logistics costs of $2,000-2,500 per container and longer shipping routes via the Cape of Good Hope, they maintained profitability through premium pricing in European markets, where their grapes command higher rates due to superior quality and higher sugar content. Their export volume reached 2.67 lakh tonnes of fresh grapes in the 2022-23 financial year, with prices trending 20% higher than the previous season. The company accounts for approximately 17% of India's grape exports and operates in 42 countries, with a particularly strong presence in European markets including the Netherlands, Lithuania, and the UK. To benefit their farmers in India, they cultivate varieties patented in the USA and Chile and export them to other countries. Sahyadri Farms has marketed two new varieties, which have received a good response from the domestic markets. At the farm gate, these varieties have sold for over Rs 230/kg with domestic traders reportinggood returns from sales.

Thecompanyprovidesitsfarmermemberswithaccesstoregenerativeagricultural practices, high-quality equipment, and a digital platform that offers real-time information about climate conditions, high-yield crop varieties, and market access. They have implemented IoT devices and digitalized farming practices to maintain quality and traceability for every grape box. The organization has also invested in advanced infrastructure, including sophisticated packhouses, residue testing facilities, and laboratories for comprehensive testing of soil, water, leaf, and petiole samples. Through initiatives like the Sahyadri Rural Development Foundation and 'The Juice Farm' store, they continue to drive positive change in the agricultural sector while maintaining their position as a leading grape exporter to Europe. Sahyadri Farms a unique company, owned and managed by small farmers, is India's largest grape exporter, transforming farmers in Nashik into millionaires by turning their "grapes of wrath" into an export export cup of gold (The Print, 2023).

Case study 2 : Mahindra Agri

Mahindra Agri has a long history of supporting farmers globally. As India's leading tractor manufacturer, the company has played a pivotal role in advancing agricultural mechanization. Recognizing the challenges and opportunities in India's agriculture, Mahindra identified the need for an integrated approach that combined various agricultural interventions to enhance exports. Guided by its vision to "Enhance farmer prosperity through Agri solutions," Mahindra Agri is dedicated to transforming farmers' lives through its unique products, services, and agricultural initiatives focused on grape exports.

Mahindra Agri has significantly contributed to the fruit export segment through its Saboro brand. The brand ensures premium quality by implementing rigorous selection, harvesting, and sorting processes, making Indian grapes competitive in global markets. The company exports White Seedless grape varieties such as Thompson and Sonaka, as well as Black Seedless varieties like Jumbo, Sharad, and Krishna. One of the most pressing challenges faced by grape farmers is market linkage, farmers struggle with middlemen, fluctuating prices, and inadequate infrastructure. Additionally, maintaining acceptable residue levels and ensuring compliance with international standards remain key hurdles. To address these issues, Mahindra focused on its fruit export business exemplifies the 'Driving Positive Change' pillar of their Rise philosophy, benefiting over 800 grape farmers in Nasik, Baramati, and Sangli in Maharashtra. The company has helped these farmers improve their exportable yield and access lucrative foreign markets, resulting in a 2X to 3X income growth for many. For example, Mahindra Agri assisted Baramati region farmers in producing high-quality black grapes after a poor 2018 export season and expanded their market reach to underexplored areas like China and Malaysia. The company supplies approximately 30 importers and 10 global supermarket chains. Mahindra exports grapes from India to various countries, including the UK, Russia, Canada, China, and Southeast Asia. At its peak, they exported 888 containers of grapes from India, primarily to Europe. In the past two years, Mahindra has expanded its export markets to China, Malaysia, Russia, Thailand, and Canada while diversifying grape varieties.

Mahindra operates a cutting-edge packhouse in Nashik, incorporating the latest cold chain management technology to ensure fresh and high-quality grapes reach global customers. The company's consistent quality under the Saboro brand is a result of strong farmer relationships and extensive support services. Through the KSKT (Khet se Khalayan Tak) program, Mahindra educates grape farmers on market quality requirements and provides the necessary support to meet these standards. These initiatives have benefited over 300 farmers, enabling them to adopt better techniques and improve yield quality. The company employs a team of agronomists and foreign experts to guide farmers throughout the production cycle. Mahindra sources grapes from over 10 packhouses in Nashik, Narayangaon, Baramati, Tuljapur, and Sangli. This diversified sourcing approach extends the supply window and provides farmers with broader market access. Mahindra & Mahindra's integrated approach to grape exports, advanced facilities, and commitment to sustainability have significantly impacted Indian agriculture. By providing farmers with market access, agronomic support, and world-class infrastructure, Mahindra continues to help Indian grape farmers thrive in an increasingly globalized market.

Conclusion

India's grape industry has experienced significant growth from 2004 to 2023, with substantial increases in area, production, consumption, and exports. Fresh grape exports have shown remarkable growth and market development, driven by improved farming techniques, early market entry, and strong demand in international markets. However, dried grape exports have faced more volatility and lower market presence. India has opportunities to enhance its global market presence, particularly by addressing quality standards, improving logistics and targeting high-potential international markets across both fresh and dried grape products. Exporters should work on meeting the stringent quality requirements and food safety standards of developed markets. Currently, India remains a net importer of dried grapes despite being a major producer of fresh grapes. Given the rising domestic demand and there should be a balanced approach to serving both export and domestic markets. There needs to be greater emphasis on value addition through processing, particularly in the dried grapes segment. Investment in processing infrastructure and technology could help capture more value from the grape supply chain and reduce the trade deficit in processed products. The development of Grape Net by APEDA has been instrumental in addressing pesticide residue issues and enhancing the traceability of grape exports, ensuring compliance with international standards and boosting demand. The Grape Net should be further enhanced with artificial intelligence and blockchain technology to improve forecasting and quality assurance. The Sahyadri Farms and Mahindra Agri have played pivotal roles in transforming the grape export sector, providing innovative practices, advanced facilities, global market access and improved the livelihoods of small farmers. The government should invest in developing new grape varieties and help smaller farmers adopt better farming techniques to promote sustainable agricultural practices to meet global export market demand. Additionally, there should be increased investment in post-harvest infrastructure, including modern packhouses and cold chain facilities, to maintain quality during transit and reduce losses. Finally, fostering strong collaborations between farmers, exporters, and government agencies will drive innovation and growth, ensuring India's competitive edge in the global grape market.

References

Aneja, Ranjan (2017). Trends and export competitiveness of major horticulture crops in India. Asian J. Hort., 12(1) : 111-116, DOI : 10.15740/HAS/TAJH/12.1/111-116.

APEDA (2025a), "Grapes" Agricultural and Processed Food Products Development Authority. available at https://www.apeda.gov.in/Grapes

APEDA (2025b), "GrapeNet" Agricultural and Processed Food Products Development Authority.availableathttps://traceability.apeda.gov.in/APEDATrustChain/GrapeNet

APEDA (Agricultural and Processed Food Products Export Development Authority) (2020a), "Report and database 2020", available at: http://apeda.gov.in/apedawebsite/six_head_product/FFV.htm#:-:text5During%202019%2D20%2C%20India%20 exported,4%2C350.13%20crores%2F%20608.48%20USD%20Millions.

APEDA (Agricultural and Processed Food Products Export Development Authority) (2020b), "Grapes report", available at: https://agriexchange.apeda.gov.in/Weekly_eReport/Grapes_Report_ Updated.pdf.

Bhattacharyya (2011) "Revealed Comparative Advantage and Competitiveness: A Case Study for India in Horticultural Products" International Conference on Applied Economics – ICOAE 2011

Bung, P. (2012). Indian fruit processing industry: import and export analysis. DHARANA-Bhavan's International Journal of Business, 71-85.

Chetia, A., Chavan, R. V., & Bharati, S. V. (2022). "Export profile and trade direction of fresh grapes from India: Markov chain approach". Pharma Innovation, 11(12), 1831-1836.

Das, A., Kumar, N. R. and Rani, P. (2016), "Growth, Instability and Forecast of Marine Products Export from India", Indian Journal of Fisheries. 63(4): 112-117.

Das K (2008). Coping with SPS Challenges in India: WTO and Beyond. Journal of International Economic Law, 11 (4): 971–1019.

ESCAP, U. (2015). Electronic traceability of agricultural products in India: the case of GrapeNet.

Export-Import Bank of India. (2014). Fresh Grapes-Export Potential from India. VOL. XVIII ISSUE II

FAOSTAT(2024),FoodandAgricultureOrganizationStatistics,availableat https://www.fao.org/faostat/en/#data/QCL

Government of India (2017). Horticultural Statistics at a Glance, 2017. Ministry of Agriculture and Farmers Welfare. New Delhi

Goyal T M, Mukherjee A, and Kapoor A (2017). India's exports of food products: Food safety related issues and way forward. Working Paper No. 345. Indian Council for Research on International Economic Relations.

https://indianexpress.com/article/lifestyle/food-wine/grapes-india-types-colour-health-benefits-storage-7170303/

Idris S, A Singh and K V Praveen (2015). Trade competitiveness and impact of food safety regulations on market access of India's horticultural trade. Agricultural Economics Research Review, Vol. 28, pp. 301-309, doi: 10.5958/0974-0279.2016.00009.4.

Indian express (2024). Indian grapes a hit in European markets, pushes exports up. Available at https://indianexpress.com/article/cities/pune/indian-grapes-hit-european-market-exports-9214060/

ITC (2024), "Trade database", International Trade Centre, Geneva, available at: https://www.trademap.org/Country_SelProductCountry_TS.aspx?nvpm= 1%7c699%7c%7c%7c%7c080620%7c%7c%7c6% 7c1%7c1%7c2%7c2%7c1%7c2%7c1% 7c1%7c1

Kearney, J., 2010. Food consumption trends and drivers. Philosophical Transactions of The Royal Society B: Biological Sciences 365(1554), 2793–2807.

Kumar, A. S., & Devaraj, M. (2020). "Export performance of grapes in India". The Journal of Research ANGRAU, 48(1), 37-45.

Kumar, Praduman and Mittal, Surabhi (2003).Crop diversification in India: Analysis by state and farm size group. Agricultural Situation in India. Special Number, August 2003. Directorate of Economics and Statistics, Ministry of Agriculture, Government of India, pp 273-280.

Lalitha, N. (2019). Can farmer producer organisations transform the small holder farming in India? A case study of Sahyadri Farmers Producer Co. Ltd. Nashik, Maharashtra. Pathways for Changing Rural Landscape, 49(1-2), 117.

Mahindraagribusiness(2025)."GrapesExport".Availableathttps://www.mahindraagri.com/our-businesses/fruits-exports-grapes/

Mahindra Rise (2021). "Driving Farm Prosperity Through Technology". Available at https://www.mahindra.com/blogs/driving-farm-prosperity-through-technology

Mamta Saxena (2014), "Indian Horticulture Database 2014, National Horticulture Board, Ministry of Agriculture, Government of India, 2014

Mukherjee A, Goyal T, Miglani S, and Kapoor A (2019). SPS barriers to India's agriculture export learning from the EU experiences in SPS and food safety standards. Indian Council for Research on International Economic Relations.

Mushair, H., Muruganandhi, D., & Rohini, A. (2020). "Export performance and trade direction of fresh and dried grapes (Raisin): evidence from Afghanistan". Journal of Economics, Management and Trade, 26(4), 37-44.

NHB (2010). Indian horticulture database. National Horticultural Board. Ministry of Agriculture, Government of India.

Nisar, U., Yongtong, M., & Kumar, N. R. (2020). "A competitive analysis of Indian fish export to USA: Growth, performance, comparative advantages and instability". Indian Journal of Geo Marine Sciences. Vol. 49 (05), May 2020, pp. 790-797

Nithin, K. N. (2016). "Production and export performance of grapes from India: An econometric analysis". Research Journal of Agricultural Sciences, 7, 143-146.

Prakash Mokashi, Hosamani SB. (2014). Direction of trade analysis of Indian grapes. International Journal of Commerce and Business Management. Vol 7(1):105 109.

Raman, M.S., Pant, D.K., Singh, A. and Kumar, R. (2023). Competitiveness of Fruits' and Vegetables' Exports from India. Econ. Aff., 68(03): 1379-1386.

Renjini, V. R. (2024). "Export of Fruits from India: Status and Challenges". Indian Journal of Agricultural Marketing, 38(2), 87-96.

Sahyadri farms (2025)."Grapes". Available at https://www.sahyadrifpc.com/core-crops#:~:text=2%20of%208.,Grapes,on%20more%20than%205%2C000%20acres.

Sharma, V. P., & Jain, D. (2011). High-value agriculture in India: Past trends and future prospects.

Shikhamany, S. D (n.d.). "Grape production in India". National Research Centre for Grapes. https://www.fao.org/4/x6897e/x6897e06.htm#:~:text=Cultivated%20grapes%20are%20believed%20to,King%20Mohammed%2Dbin%2DTughlak.

Sharma, A. K., & Adulse, P. G. (2007). Raisin production in India. Pune: NRC for grapes, 1-5.

Sihmar, R. 2014. Growth and Instability in Agricultural Production in Haryana: A District level Analysis. Int. J. Sci. Res. Publ., 4(7): 1-12

Singh, Ritambhara & Khanna, Vishita. (2021). Emerging marketing trends in fruits and vegetables. 677-705

Somkuwar, R. G., Naik, S., Sharma, A. K., & Bhange, M. A. (2019). Performance of grape varieties grown under tropical regions for raisin yield and quality. Indian Journal of Horticulture, 76(02), 355-357.

Suman, J., Shekhawat, P.S., Jain, S. and Verma, D.K. (2022). Performance of Growth, Instability and Comparative Advantage in Export of Fruits and Vegetables from India. Agro Economist - An International Journal, 09(04): 299-305.

The Economic times (2018). "Sahyadri Farms emerges as India's largest grape exporter of 2018-19". Available at https://economictimes.indiatimes.com/news/economy/agriculture/sahyadri-farms-emerges-as-indias-largest-grape-exporter-of-201819/articleshow/ 70058281.cms?utm_source=contentofinterest&utm_medium=text&utm_campaign=cppst.

The Print (2023). "Nashik's Sahyadri Farms turns grapes of wrath to export cup of gold. Farmers are millionaires". Available at https://theprint.in/feature/nashiks-sahyadri-farm-turns-grapes-of-wrath-to-export-cup-of-gold-farmers-are-millionaires/1501038/

Thulasiram, R., & Alagumani, T. (2015). An economic analysis on export performance of fresh grapes from India. Indian Journal of Agricultural Marketing, 29(3), 33-39.

Tong, G.; Hong, R.; Shi, L. (2023). The Growth Effect and Its Influencing Factors: Empirical Evidence Regarding China's Fruit and Vegetable Exports to RCEP Countries. Agriculture 2023, 13, 1908. https:// doi.org/10.3390/agriculture13101908

Umali Deininger D and Sur M (2007) Food safety in a globalizing world: opportunities and challenges for India. Agricultural Economics, 37:135-147

United States Department of Agriculture (2024)."Fresh apples, grapes, and pears: World markets and trade". Foreign Agricultural Service, 1-10.

USAID-funded Commercial Horticulture and Agricultural Marketing Program (2016). Farm to Market Guide – Best Practices for GRAPE Production and Marketing in Afghanistan.

Vasavada, K. M., & Shiyani, R. L. (2023), "Growth and Instability of Exports of Vegetable Products from India". Indian Journal of Agricultural Marketing, 37(1), 161-169.

Venkitasamy, C., Zhao, L., Zhang, R., & Pan, Z. (2019). Grapes. In Integrated processing technologies for food and agricultural by-products (pp. 133-163). Academic Press.

Index